HUMAN DISCOURSE

HUMAN DISCOURSE

The Bridge to Collective Mind and Spirit

By

Nicholas Blakiston

I fell through a cloud and was laughing aloud
as I felt the mist tickle my face.
I soared through the skies yelling triumphant cries
and encountered an angel of grace.

The love that then filled me has ever since thrilled me.
A longing has captured my soul.
The future will greet us and more love will meet us
and humans will then be made whole.

For I have surrendered - my heart has been rendered
as helpless as infant in womb.
Come join me - we'll travel and pain will unravel
and fear will lay rest in a tomb.

Human Discourse

ISBN: 9798779240147

www.humandiscourse.com

One can resist the invasion of an army, but one cannot resist the invasion of ideas.
Victor Hugo

Acknowledgements

As I sit here in the middle of the night on the verge of completion of this book, I am amazed at how much has fallen into place to lead to its creation. I have had several rare experiences in my life that have combined to place me in the unique position to produce this book. I cannot attribute this to chance and must therefore attribute it to the work of a higher power, whom I will refer to throughout this book as God. And, it is to God that my first acknowledgement is made, for without this incredible universe he has given us to work and play in, there would no book, nor any reason to write one. Thank you to God for all of the miracles you've placed in my life and in this universe.

I must also thank my schoolteachers, my parents, and the other adults who brought me into this world. It is through their toil that I was able to survive my early years, through their kindness that I have been able to survive my recent years, and through their wisdom that I have sought out wisdom for myself.

I would also like to thank the spiritual companions I have made along the way, including most especially Kevin, Chuck, Bill, Marla, Ivie, and Gwen.

I would like to thank those I've worked with for teaching me discipline, patience, perseverance, nuclear power plant operations and accounting.

I would like to thank all of my friends, but most especially those who have stuck with me emotionally through my most difficult moments these past few years including my father, Steve, Marla, Melissa, Courtney, Kes, Ivie, Ty and Zeb.

It appears some individuals are appearing on multiple occasions here.

I would like to thank the crowd at the casino for showing me what I don't want, and I would like to thank the crowd at my improv class for providing me with a measure of joy in what has been a trying time. Thank you especially to our instructor Joe who keeps good order in the class and doesn't let me get away with breaking the rules.

I would also like to thank the countless humans on this planet who have toiled day in and day out for the hope of a better tomorrow. I extend my hand to you in love and hope you will join me on a journey through the reality we live in and towards that better tomorrow.

I would like to thank all the free thinkers, the rebels, and all of those who have challenged the social, cultural and intellectual norms of their day at the expense of their own joy, reputations, relationships, funding, health, desires, and occasionally lives. Your sacrifices for the sake of seeking truth have been an inspiration to me and you have helped me complete the incredible human discourse that has given me the material to write this book.

Preface

I first set out to write a book in the fall of 2017, following inspiration I gained from a George Carlin skit in which he was doing a mock presidential election. With memories of the 2016 presidential debates between Hillary Clinton and Donald Trump fresh in my mind, I became convinced that I could answer the questions they were asked better than the candidates did. As a result of this, the first version of this book was no more than a question-and-answer section based on the three debates they had.

As I set out to answer these questions, the topic of global warming came up and I realized I had insufficient knowledge to answer the question asked. I decided to watch an episode of The Cosmos, a television documentary narrated by Neil deGrasse Tyson, a famous astrophysicist. It had been modeled after Carl Sagan's previous series of the same name and in the episode I watched, they broke down the global warming phenomenon including the mechanism by which greenhouse gases trap heat in the Earth's atmosphere and the warming effect it was having on our planet. They showed me scenes of environmental destruction that was occurring because of this phenomenon, and successfully convinced me that it was a real issue of concern.

This had a major impact on me, not just because of what it informed me of regarding the specific global warming issue, but because of what it informed me of within my own psyche. I had heard many people discuss global warming, but I realized I had never paid much attention to what they had said. How was it possible that I had survived so long in my life without even becoming fully aware of the issue, and without even having heard the basic explanation of how greenhouse gases trap heat in the atmosphere?

I realized that up until that point in my life, I had listened to other people with the wrong intentions. Instead of listening to understand them and their concerns, I had listened from a place of trying to disprove their claims. I was more interested in what I understood than what they understood and approached discourse with the intention to convince other people of what I knew.

In a flash, it occurred to me that this was the wrong way to approach discourse. What good did it do me to focus on what I already knew? I already had that knowledge and was not benefitting from focusing on it. I could only reap a benefit if I instead listened and sought to understand what others knew, but that I did not.

Since that moment of awakening, I have sought to approach every interaction with the intention to understand, with a diminished interest in being understood. Doing so has led me down a path of rapid intellectual advancement and inspired me to come up with the name of my book, Human Discourse.

Prior to my moment of awakening, I had spent a great deal of time studying economics and understood economic principles in a very grounded way. This understanding has helped steady me as additional information has come into my awareness, and the solutions I've come up with have had to be integrated with that understanding. After four years, many discarded drafts, and a massive journey of intellectual, emotional, and spiritual growth, I am presenting in this book the best solutions I can come up with for our society.

While writing this book, it has become apparent to me that the solutions we seek need to be creative and specific, rather than appealing to vague principles that may be defined differently by different people. We need specific actionable steps we can take, as individuals and as a society, to correct what is wrong in our world and to build a new and free one. It is not enough to say government is bad, for it is necessary to define both government and for whom in that sentence. It is also not enough because government as it exists provides many services upon which we are dependent, and an orderly transition to a free society needs to occur. It is also not enough because merely blaming the government is doing what so many others have done, highlighting a problem without providing any real solutions. This is a book of solutions.

Some of these solutions are complex and while I've attempted to tie up every loose end and address as many potential circumstances as possible in this book, I am only one man and I lack the foresight to envision every possible circumstance that may occur in a universe of infinite possibilities. I also lack the technical expertise that will be required to smoothly transition every industry from our legacy system to the new and free one. This book is intended only as a starting point in the discussion and I am open to discussion as we revise these solutions to consider parameters I had not previously considered.

With that said, I do go into depth on many topics and propose specific ideas that address the lion's share of the major societal concerns we have. My book can act as a starting template for us to move forward peacefully as a society and should offer hope to a population that to a great extent is becoming more hopeless by the day.

I have not become a global warming expert since I watched that documentary and I am aware that greatly diverse viewpoints remain on this issue. While I will assume for the purposes of this book that the issue is a real one, I will not demand that anyone contribute to addressing that issue who is not interested in doing so. I will show how societal and ecological issues can be resolved even if not everyone in society is concerned about them and how individual charity, rather than taxation, is the best mechanism by which people can address those causes that speak to them most loudly.

Table of Contents

Part I: Collapse and Transition

Paradise

Once, an ancient man named Adam lived in Paradise.
Aside him lived a lovely madam: noble, nude and nice.
In their garden's splendid beauty, a tree of knowledge stood.
It seemed so lush and fruity and would teach them bad from good.

But its fruit brought them disaster: they hid themselves in shame.
Fear became a loathsome master: they started placing blame.
Despite the fact inside the garden, evil had no hold,
hearts began to harden and their warmth gave way to cold.

For eons, we've all lived like this, yet always the allure:
a longing for eternal bliss, a love that's true and pure.
But our efforts seem to fail and pain resumes once more.
The secret is we're trapped in jail and must within explore.

Our prison walls are made of fears which truly just are lies.
Examined, soon the truth appears and fear fades from our eyes.
Beyond the walls, the sun shines well: it shined on Adam too.
And Paradise, from whence he fell, still beckons me and you.

Pandora's Box

In Greek mythology, humans once lived in a Golden Age where suffering did not exist. In this world of bliss, a titan named Epimetheus resided with a wondrous angelic companion named Pandora. The gods presented them with a box, which they were instructed not to open. Curiosity eventually got the best of Pandora and she chanced a peek. Disaster soon followed as troubles escaped the box and made their way into the world.

Muslim, Jewish, and Christian scriptures recount the story of Adam and Eve who also lived in a state of paradise, known as the Garden of Eden. Scripture recounts that God offered this paradise to man and woman but that they chose to eat from a tree of knowledge, one which would spell disaster for their species and result in their fall from grace.

Eastern philosophies also describe a state of paradise, but it is seen as a futuristic state that is achieved through the suffering of lifetimes. Buddhists attempt to reach a state of Nirvana whereby suffering is transcended while Hindus attempt to escape the cycle of rebirth to enter a state of perfection known as Moksha.

Among all of these philosophies, there is a common theme that a greater state of existence is possible than what we experience here in this reality. This higher experience is no myth but is something I briefly experienced during the summer months of 2018, when I came to believe that true love had found me. It had, but it would demand an arduous journey to ground itself within the society I live in.

During the time since then, our world has been experiencing a great spiritual transition. Love has gained a foothold here, but it has been surrounded by ignorance and cruelty. Yet it has worked, minute by minute, to spread itself across the face of our planet and to upheave the structures that have enslaved us as a species.

The coronavirus pandemic and related hysteria is but a symptom of this greater spiritual transition. Old lines of reasoning are being questioned, secrets are being exposed, and men are being made. We are on a journey towards freedom and while the scenery of this journey may disturb us, our ultimate destination will eventually materialize.

In this book, I will examine the world as it exists today and discuss a path forward so that we may complete this transition and joy can materialize in this world. This discussion will look at the various economic markets necessary to a functioning society and how government restraints of those markets can be removed so they can operate efficiently and effectively. I will discuss the spiritual aspects of our transition, including the return of Christ, the reappearance of mystical beings who have fled our perception in fear, our connection with the greater galactic hoard, and individual action steps people can take as we collectively experience this transition.

A lesser-known part of the Greek myth of Pandora's Box is that in addition to the troubles that were unleashed upon the world was a little fairy named Hope. My own hope is that everyone reading this will embark upon a journey to catch her with me. As we do so, may that little fairy grow into something powerful and majestic, and help to banish our troubles from this very troubled world.

Morality

Life outcomes are a combination of good fortune and merit, although even merit can ultimately be derived from good fortune. Consider the following scenarios:

1.　A person gets rich because they understand how money works, but they are still fortunate to have acquired the knowledge that later enabled them to become rich.

2.　A person worked hard and got rich from doing so, but they are still fortunate to live in a society where that economic opportunity existed for them and where their body would allow them to perform that labor while maintaining its good health over a period of decades.

3.　A person spent a lot of time in the gym getting into shape but is fortunate their other responsibilities and desires in life were minimal enough to allow them the time for this effort.

For any success, a person should not credit only their own efforts, but also the many factors outside of their control that aligned to enable that success.

Failure is the same way. Perhaps a person spent just as much time working hard and studying money as the wealthy people from #1 and #2 above but worked in a career that would become obsolete during their tenure, and studied financial information presented by people who themselves did not understand money. Perhaps a person spent just as much time as the person in #3 in the gym but an unfortunate accident paralyzed the individual, negating their years of effort.

Because of this combination of factors within and beyond an individual's control, it is foolhardy to leap to judgements about other individuals based on superficial metrics such as bank account balance or body-mass index. Until we have walked in that individual's shoes or heard a first-hand account regarding their behavior, we cannot hope to understand every factor that led to their circumstances. To become an effective judge, we must develop empathy to discover and understand the reasons for the behavior being judged.

Judgement is necessary at times. If I'm an employer looking to hire someone, I must judge the merit of the various candidates applying for the position. If I am deciding who to leave my inheritance to, I must perform a judgement. If I am deciding who to date, I must perform a judgement. Ultimately, not everyone can be a winner and we need a mechanism to separate the wheat from the chaff.

The key to good judgement is not judging the specific behavior of an individual but judging the reasons such behavior is undertaken. It is easy to define a particular action as good or bad but there are frequently exceptions to the defined rule. We can say it is wrong to kill someone but if a maniac is killed while committing a mass shooting, we can argue that a greater good was accomplished by taking out the maniac, despite the one who took them out having violated the basic rule of not killing anyone.

Once we have made our judgements, it is up to us to administer the gifts or punishments that we feel befit that judgement. A gift is an act of kindness intended to benefit someone else while a punishment is an act of cruelty intended to hurt someone else.

The same action can be a gift or a punishment, depending upon the motivation of the actor. If I cut off communication with someone because I feel my communicating with them will enable behavior that is destructive to them and others, my behavior is motivated by kindness and can be considered a gift, even though the recipient may not immediately see it as a gift.

If my decision to cut the person off is instead motivated by a desire to hurt that individual because I don't like them, the same action that was intended as a gift can now be considered a punishment.

An action doesn't necessarily have to be either a reward or a punishment. It may be that I am cutting them off because it serves my own motives, and I haven't considered the effect it will have on them. But, if this is my motivation, I should question my lack of empathy. A lack of consideration of the consequences of our actions on others may result in just as much harm to them as an intentional punishment, and I see no excuse for it. Whenever my behavior has an impact on others, I should consider that impact and ensure that my motives are good.

I find it unnecessary to administer punishments to others, and the entirety of my action towards others at the current time is either neutral or intended as a gift. Punishment is administered to attempt to satisfy resentment and I find resentment to be an unhealthy spiritual condition to live in. Just because I judge the behavior of another as destructive, it doesn't mean I have to punish them for participating in it. I might take action that is harmful to them as a sacrifice for the greater good (e.g., taking out the mass shooter) but my intention will not be punishment. I may offer them a gift that may not feel good, such as the truth, and I may withhold gifts from them that I find others to be more worthy of, such as my company or respect. But I leave punishment up to God.

It seems that God designed this universe in such a way that on a long enough time horizon, punishments arise from the natural world without human action. If a person makes a poor investment decision, they are punished with a loss of their investment. If a person makes a poor marriage decision, they are punished with an unhappy life. If a person decides to be cruel, they ultimately discover that others do not like them, and only abide by their wishes out of fear.

It is my personal belief that God's justice extends beyond this life, and I leave it up to him to punish the sins of humanity to the extent that he deems it necessary. Jesus instructed us to love one another, and it is my belief that this is the optimal behavior for a human.

Moral differences

In the previous section, I presented my personal moral views, that people should act with kindness and present gifts to reward good behavior, rather than using punishments to punish bad behavior. However, I am just a single individual and as I have engaged with others on this planet, it has come into my awareness that different people hold different moral ideas. Libertarians frequently refer to the "non-aggression principle" as a basis of morality but just because they believe this to be a just principle doesn't mean others on this planet agree. In fact, many will likely argue over what aggression even means within the context of that principle. A Marxist might argue that hiring someone for a wage while keeping a profit is a form of aggression. I am not here to settle these moral differences, for the reality of absolute moral truth is mostly irrelevant as far as crafting a path forward. The relevant question is and has always been not who is more moral, but who has the power to enforce that which they believe to be moral.

As a libertarian myself, I appreciate the spirit behind the "non-aggression principle" but recognize that my appreciation of this principle by itself has done little to help those who are being confined, abused, raped, stolen from, and killed by governments and others in this world. There are those in this world who have justified such behaviors to themselves, and my focus is on convincing them to end those behaviors with an acknowledgement of the reality that no matter what moral appeals I make, they are unlikely to agree with me.

As such, this book will not discuss morality much beyond what I have discussed in these two sections. The focus will instead be on actionable steps that can be taken by the people of this world to improve their own lives and the lives of those around them.

Reality

A plan of action must start with an acknowledgement of the reality that currently exists. I have already mentioned the reality of the moral differences in this world, but there are other aspects of reality that are also worthy of note:

1. The United States dollar is likely to soon become a worthless currency. At this point, most libertarians and other free-minded individuals understand this. If you do not, I highly recommend checking out my website www.humandiscourse.com where you can find many resources to provide explanations of this crisis. I highly recommend the work of Peter Schiff in particular, who is linked on that website.

2. When the United States dollar collapses, many individuals within the United States will become unable to purchase food or other basic necessities and have a high likelihood of resorting to violence out of desperation to feed themselves.

3. A significant number of individuals within the United States own gold, land, firearms, and other hard assets that will increase their chances of survival in the days to come.

4. Many individuals within the United States have taken, or will take, supposed "vaccinations" against the supposed "coronavirus". While many theories exist regarding the extent of the medical damage these individuals can expect to suffer from this decision, the ultimate death numbers are as yet unknown.

5. Many individuals around the world have been socially distancing and wearing facemasks to prevent the spread of germs for the past couple of years, a phenomenon that may result in widespread outbreaks of disease caused by immunity debt if these individuals ever re-integrate with the greater society.

6. Many individuals in the United States are currently confined in prison, and many are there for committing victimless crimes.

7. A concentrated effort is happening globally to wage war against the unvaccinated through economic sanctions, social

9

isolation, and shunning. In Australia, the spearhead of this effort, quarantine camps are being used which seem to bear a strong resemblance to death camps such as those reported to have been used by the Nazi forces against Jews, homosexuals and other supposedly undesirable groups during World War 2.

8. The United States government and their allies in state and local governments, the mainstream media, the Big Tech companies, the Big Pharma companies, the military industrial complex, the big banks, and the other corporations currently wielding power in the United States seem willing to go to any lengths necessary to maintain their positions of power in this world.

9. There are authoritarian governments around the world that have oppressed the human population. In many areas, war and famine are ravaging populations as people suffer under this tyranny.

10. Many people are concerned about a global warming crisis. Some of these individuals are also likely to believe that human depopulation is the only method by which this crisis can be addressed. The coronavirus hysteria may be an attempt to initiate this depopulation agenda.

Collapse

Of all the facts mentioned in the previous section, the collapse of the United States dollar is the most prominent. This will be the most significant economic event in human history. Billions of people who have relied upon our current systems of government for their existence will find themselves with few assets, no source of income, and little chance of survival.

It is the very magnitude of this event that I expect to inspire hopelessness within a population once placing its hope in government, and that may allow the freedom movement the opportunity to turn the corner in the global struggle against tyranny.

When I was 24 years old, I was at the tail end of my 6-year naval career and found myself struggling with alcoholism to the degree that I could not hold a job or maintain any meaningful social connections. I had experienced many negative consequences from my drinking including multiple hospital visits, arrests, loss of rank, money, friendships, and a 30-day trip to the Navy's brig.

The U.S. Navy kindly placed me in two alcohol treatment centers during my enlistment and at these centers, I was provided with resources and suggestions as to how I might recover from my alcoholic condition. Despite this, I failed to take any of the suggestions offered and instead wrote them off mentally without attempting them. To me, my problem was alcohol, and the solution was a simple as not drinking. I had not adequately listened to understand the nature of alcoholism, nor the spiritual sickness that underlies the condition of the active alcoholic.

Despite a fairly checkered naval career, I was discharged honorably in August of 2006. While I may have been separated from the Navy, I remained attached to alcohol. On January 11, 2007, after another disastrous night of attempting to control and enjoy it, I became convinced that I was powerless over my alcoholism and would keep on drinking to the bitter end. I became entirely hopeless, and it was this hopelessness that prompted me finally take the suggestions I had heard at the treatment centers. I became determined to jump through every hoop of supposed alcohol recovery before I arrived at my inevitable early grave. I did not believe the suggestions would work, but I wanted to show the people in this world that I had done everything possible to resolve my alcoholism prior to my inevitable demise. I might lose my life, but I'd be damned if people didn't think I at least tried.

Through an undertaking of the suggestions I had heard, I became connected with a spiritual group of recovered alcoholics and amongst that group, I discovered hope. I listened to the accounts of others who had once been as hopeless as me and I saw them standing up with months or even years of sobriety behind them. I soon discovered that these individuals had contacted God and that he had rescued them from a hopeless condition similar to that in which I now found myself.

Their recovery offered me hope, but it gave me no guarantees. Despite convincing me that there was indeed a higher power named God, I did not know how this higher power would respond to my offering my own life and will over to his care. I expected that based on some of the things I'd done in my life, there was a good chance he would strike me dead where I stood. Despite this, I was willing to give myself to him, because he was my only hope. With God, the future was uncertain, but without him, it was certain defeat.

I relate this story because uncertainty is a curious phenomenon among our species. It seems that if the status quo remains bearable, uncertainty is seen as a threat, and individuals seek to avoid it at all costs. It is only once the status quo becomes unbearable that uncertainty no longer inspires fear, but instead inspires hope.

Many people have avoided listening to those of us warning about the forthcoming collapse of the U.S. dollar, and the implications of that event, because they fear looking into an uncertain future. Without acknowledging reality, they can carry about their daily lives as if nothing is amiss. They can live in comfort and avoid the discomfort that an honest look at reality would bring. I expect their condition to continue right up until the status quo becomes unbearable.

The collapse of the US dollar is just the keystone in the collapse of a massive credit bubble that has mispriced virtually every market we have. When this credit bubble collapses, Americans will discover that not only have the government payments they have relied upon for income become unable to purchase enough food to feed them, but also that many companies have only existed as an ancillary to the government structure that has existed. Without government credit, these ventures will also fail.

Individuals will take massive losses in their retirement accounts as many stocks become worthless and the bond market entirely collapses. Banks will fail, insurance companies will fail, pension funds will fail, and the social security trust fund will become essentially worthless. Residential and commercial real estate prices will collapse, individual savings will be destroyed, and people will wake up to discover themselves in a harsh reality where they have no food, no income, and no safety net to catch them.

Once this event happens, the status quo is unlikely to remain bearable. I expect people to feel utterly hopeless, in such a way as I felt when it seemed there was no escape from my alcoholism. And just as this hopelessness prompted me to act with an uncertain outcome, the hopelessness that will exist in the wake of the dollar's collapse may prompt a sort-of communal spiritual experience whereby those who have been shutting themselves off from reality are finally forced to face it, and to grab onto whatever hope they can. And the uncertainty of a future free from government that has for so long inspired fear amongst the population may finally instead inspire hope.

Throughout the rest of this book, I will discuss actionable steps that we can take in the wake of the dollar's collapse to not only survive, but to rebuild our economy and our lives from the ground up. It will be a massive undertaking, but I will not underestimate the power of human effort and ingenuity to carry us through to a brighter future. Our species has found ways to adapt and survive for thousands of years, despite all that governments have done to impede that progress. With the restraints of government removed, free humans will ascend from the depths of the hell of ignorance they've been living in to ultimately create heaven on Earth.

Transition of Government

Throughout this book, I will have a U.S. centric focus, even though our ultimate destination is global freedom. As a U.S. citizen and resident, I am most familiar with our own government and the conditions that exist within this country. I am not in the business of telling other countries what to do, and while I feel compassion for those throughout the world oppressed by other governments, my belief is that the best thing we can do for those individuals is to create a free society here. Doing so will give people around the world an example to follow as well as a potential refuge to flee to. Having a free economy here will create prosperity and with that prosperity, the individuals in this society can be empowered to undertake efforts to help those others oppressed around the world. In a later section, I will discuss foreign affairs in more detail.

We currently operate under a complex system of government laws and regulations but such things, up to and including amendments to the U.S. constitution, can happen quickly and efficiently if we presume that a widespread spiritual awakening has happened and the population, including those currently in government, has agreed that these steps are necessary to ensure the survival of our civilization.

I am not a legal scholar, but I am confident that when everyone has the same objectives, whatever technicalities stand in the way from a legal standpoint can be dealt with. From this point forward, I will not be discussing the legal requirements necessary to achieve these objectives, but simply stating what the objectives should be. Legal scholars can figure out the specific hoops that need to be jumped through once we have consensus on the destination.

The United States consists of a federal government as well as state and territorial governments, county governments and city governments. In the wake of the dollar's collapse, all these governments will need to start taking action to prevent their citizens from perishing. Most U.S. citizens keep less than two weeks' worth of food in their home so the need for prompt and productive action will be great.

In the wake of the collapse of this credit bubble, the United States government should immediately declare the U.S. dollar and all debts payable in that currency to be worthless. While this may not seem nice to those who have savings and loans receivable payable in dollars, I am suggesting this declaration be made in the wake of a major financial catastrophe that has already rendered these assets close to worthless. Declaring them entirely worthless will save society the unnecessary headache of having to mail in worthless payments for years to come and allow us to focus our productive efforts in a more useful way.

The United States Federal government is purported to own approximately 8,000 tons of gold, but the gold reserve has not been audited in many decades. The U.S. government should immediately start accepting bids, payable in gold, to audit that gold reserve and ensure it has been kept safe from theft. Once we know how much gold is there, we can make a distribution to the population to buy them some time to survive and find gainful employment in our new economy. My suggestion is that we immediately distribute 20 percent of the gold equally amongst U.S. citizens and legal residents, the group of individuals formerly subject to the U.S. tax code.

I suggest that another 20 percent of the discovered gold should be distributed amongst the states, in pro-ration to their population, to assist them with winding down their operations. The states will then have to decide how much of this gold payment to distribute amongst the states and cities within their area. I propose that U.S. territories where the population has not been subject to the U.S. tax code also receive a portion of this 20% but to compensate for the fact their citizens have not been paying Federal tax, I suggest their disbursement only be half of what it would be based upon the same population for a state.

The U.S. tax code should be declared null and void immediately and the Federal government should immediately stop regulating industry to the greatest extent possible. For certain critical regulatory efforts such as those regulating air traffic control and nuclear power, there will need to be a well-thought out and orderly transition away from government regulation and to regulation by the new authorities established for these specific instances. These cases will be discussed in later sections but ultimately, all laws and regulations enforced by the U.S. government should be either immediately ended or immediately begin a process of transition to the private sector.

Governments will also need to transition other services they provide to private and charitably funded providers and many such services will be discussed in later sections.

The U.S. government should evaluate the price of gold in relation to other commodities and price a new U.S. dollar in gold. The old dollar should be declared worthless but pricing a new dollar in gold will help to facilitate commerce, as many technologies have been set up to transact in dollars and cents. If a store can use the same credit card machine it previously used to accept fiat dollars to now accept a payment of gold stored by a gold bank, this will greatly assist us in a smooth economic transition.

Companies and individuals who have a good reputation can assist the government in this distribution of gold to the population by setting up new gold banking systems, assisting companies in transitioning to accepting gold payments, and providing other services that will be in demand during this transition. Assuming government has done the right thing and stopped regulating the economy, they will be free to do so without having to jump through any red tape or worry about their government licensing, tax and reporting requirements. The liquidating entity of the Federal government can accept bids from such companies in pursuit of their new objectives, which will be transitioning their services to the private sector and liquidating their remaining physical assets into gold, ultimately disbursing that gold to the population and to the former states that will also be winding down their operations.

In determining who should head up the liquidation process, I suggest that the population use a democratic process to vote in the head of liquidation for each level of the former government. Candidates for such an office will need to demonstrate their ethical nature to the population, as well as a vision that they believe will serve the population's best interest.

In many circumstances, the government will be faced with the decision of immediately liquidating assets or holding assets for the purpose of attempting to achieve capital appreciation on behalf of the population. The Federal government owns a lot of land, and a lot of oil through the strategic petroleum reserve. If such assets were immediately liquidated, the liquidators may not be able to demand anything above a bargain basement price for them as they will be selling into a depressed market and flooding it with a large amount of that resource at one time. By choosing instead to liquidate its assets gradually over time, the liquidating entity may be able to demand higher market prices.

Once we have a free economy, it should be expected that the price of finite resources such as land and oil will gradually increase over time as people come up with more and more efficient and profitable uses for those resources. By using a democratic process, the citizens can listen to the arguments of those who think more assets should be liquidated versus those who think the assets should be held for a time as a speculation.

Perhaps one candidate will suggest that different citizens can make an individual determination and so those who wish for an immediate disbursement can have their share of the land or oil liquidated immediately, and their gold shipped to them. Those who prefer to hold off can allow the liquidating entity to hold those assets in trust until a future time when, hopefully, those assets have appreciated in price.

Perhaps different candidates will suggest different time horizons for how often someone may choose to liquidate their share. By offering a less frequent opportunity to choose to liquidate, large numbers of people can liquidate at once, rather than having to sell small bits of land frequently and incurring

18

additional costs. There will be many complexities in the liquidation process and many discussions will need to take place as different parties offer their perspective as to how to maximize the ultimate value of the liquidation proceeds going to the population.

Different candidates for liquidation office may propose unique and creative ideas. Perhaps one will suggest that with the large number of weapons owned by our military, they should simply be disbursed for free to individuals in our society interested in owning one. Those interested in applying for one could send in an application and presuming there are more people interested than weapons available, lotteries can be held to determine who should get a weapon. By increasing the number of weapons available in society, this will not only provide individuals with the means to protect themselves in the event any unrest occurs during our transition, but it will also place a large supply of weapons on the market that are being sold by individuals who did not care about owning a weapon and only entered the lottery so they could sell it. By decreasing the price of weapons, it will give families that were not fortunate enough to win a lottery a chance to purchase one at a lower price.

Each state, county and local government should also cease restricting economic markets and start to liquidate their assets, returning the proceeds of such liquidations to the populations formerly subject to their taxing authority. Different localities can attempt different liquidation and transition strategies, and those strategies that are successful will likely be copied by others.

While many companies may find it most convenient to accept payments in gold that are priced in dollars compatible with their legacy technology, some companies and individuals may decide they prefer to use an alternative currency such as silver, platinum, Bitcoin, or other cryptocurrencies. It's even possible that some states or cities may decide to accept these alternative currencies as payment during their liquidations which will then be transferred to their populations. People and entities should use whatever currencies they feel are most effective in facilitating the trades they wish to participate in. No government should be setting rules declaring any currency to be the only legal tender, but each government's liquidation estate can decide which currency or currencies they should accept to best accomplish their objectives of ending their operations and liquidating their assets.

Out of the original gold reserve, assuming we distribute 20 percent to the population and 20 percent to the states as I have suggested, I also suggest 10% be maintained by the Federal government for the purposes of operating capital while undertaking their process of ending their operations and liquidating their assets. I suggest the remaining 50 percent should be held in reserve for some period and then disbursed amongst the population and to the states. Because people in our society have been living in a massive credit bubble, few have learned financial responsibility and it is highly likely they will quickly blow through that first 20% disbursement. By breaking the disbursement up into annual or bi-annual payments, it will give more people a chance to survive for longer and extend the slim societal safety net for as long as possible. The timeline of distributing the remaining 50% does not have to be immediately determined and can be adjusted based on what the economy looks like in the months following the collapse.

Sound money is critical to a functioning economy and gold provides a stable foundation that individuals have returned to time and again throughout history as economic crises have occurred. It is recognized the world over for its inherent beauty, a characteristic that gives it intrinsic value and ensures it will maintain value, regardless of economic conditions. While a return to sound money is a critical step in transitioning to a functioning economy, it is but one market out of many that must be considered. Additional markets will be discussed in part II of this book.

Transition of Private Enterprise

In addition to the crises governments will face, businesses across our country will face great challenges as this economic transition occurs. With the U.S. dollar and all U.S. dollar denominated debts declared worthless, each company's equity will be worth simply the value of its tangible and intangible assets[1]. Each company's board of directors and management team will need to determine whether that company still has a going concern and how it should proceed to maximize the value its shareholders will receive. In many circumstances, it will be determined that without a centralized government, the company no longer has a place in the market. In these circumstances, the companies will need to liquidate their assets and return whatever proceeds are raised to their shareholders. They will need to inform their employees that they no longer are employed. They will need to contact their suppliers and distributors to let them know if they are being forced to break their contracts, due to the economic catastrophe.

In response to widespread liquidations going on in the absence of the former government bankruptcy court system, many services will be demanded such as people who can mediate contract disputes between parties, people who can link up buyers and sellers of liquidated assets, and so on. By having a free economy, people can offer such services without any government interference. These demands can be met efficiently while employing people and decreasing the overall level of despair that society will be experiencing in the wake of this collapse.

While many companies will likely determine to entirely liquidate, other companies will discover that their business, or at least part of their business, still has relevance in the new marketplace. These companies can determine which employees and parts of their business they should retain and some may even

---

[1] Unless they have notes receivable in a foreign currency that has retained value

expand to offer additional services they were either not able to legally offer previously or to respond to the new demands that will arise in a quickly shifting economy.

With a free market financial and banking system, many companies may decide they want to change their ownership structure by either reducing or increasing their number of shareholders, or by offering new classes of stock or partnership interests that were not previously feasible. They may decide they want to de-list from stock exchanges that they feel have become discredited and may want to list their shares for sale on new stock exchanges that are now free to compete with one another. They may want to open bank accounts with new banks, they may want to report their financial statements on a different basis of accounting than has what previously been allowed, and they may want to establish credit with new lenders.

There will be capital in society, for whoever owns gold will discover there has been a massive deflationary collapse when viewing the price of assets in terms of gold. With governments and businesses liquidating their assets, there will be many bargain-basement deals to be had and those who possess capital will start searching society for good investments. This will be a critical step in rebuilding the economy, for the capital that these individuals have can allow those in society who have good business ideas to put those ideas into action.

Part II: Markets

Phoenix Rising

A fire, if ever you sailed the sea,
is the worst kind of nautical tragedy.
The flames that burn through the skin and the flesh
can cook people sure as the fish they enmesh.

The fire that's sweeping this desolate land
s fire entrenched in a spirit's demand.
The wish for its freedom, the wish for its joy,
the wish for the knowledge it yearns to employ.

The fire that scorches the ego adrift
is one that is fueled by a once mighty rift.
The pain of the species, the horrors of hell,
unspoken tragedies casting a spell,

Lifting a human to wondrous deeds,
vanquishing fear and fulfilling our needs.
God's mighty hand is incarnate on Earth,
leading the people to wonder and mirth.

All of the madness and fear you can find,
all of it will be removed from the mind.
All of the punishment, all of the pain,
all will be healed as the fire does reign.

All of the ignorance, all of the guilt,
all will be lost as the smoke forms a quilt.
All that's within will be burned to a crisp,
the smoke will disburse until it's just a wisp.

Out of the ashes, a Phoenix will rise,
science will think this is quite a surprise.
God's mighty hand will give life to the ash,
humans will know they longer want cash.

Now they want love and the pull of the heart
is the key that unlocks and the place that we start.
We listen and do what our master demands,
the heart that's inside us wherever it lands.

We listen and learn and we tell of its love,
we tell and we give it to heaven above.
Then we are free and the rest of the tale
is one I will know when I finally sail.

Right now I'm anchored, I'm treating the wood,
I'm polishing brass 'til it's shiny and good.
The fire that's sweeping this innocent land
s one that I've been through and thus understand.

If I depart and my ship sails to sea,
won't you remember that love came to me.
Follow the plan and trust in the Lord,
he's mighty and can give a mighty reward.

Follow your heart and love with your mind,
if you do that purest joy you will find.
Give it to God and to love that's divine,
that's what I did and it's working out fine.

Security

Earlier, I discussed morality and how it seems impossible to convince anyone else that what I see as moral is truly moral. In contrast, I find myself in a world where whoever has the power to enforce their morality gets to decide which version of morality will be enforced. Power in this world is a derivative of purchasing power, for those who can purchase guns and hire people to use them are typically able to gain control of society and enforce the version of morality that they think is best.

When the current credit and U.S. dollar bubbles bursts, there will be a massive shift in purchasing power away from those who have controlled it up to this point and towards those who own gold and other hard assets that have maintained or appreciated in value. Regardless of whether the authorities of the current power structure willfully concede to a plan of government's termination and liquidation, this transfer purchasing power will occur. Even if government officials decide they will go on to the bitter end, doing everything they can to defeat those who desire to be free, they will ultimately find themselves powerless over the society they have controlled up to this point.

Once the store shelves are empty, the population will become enraged, and they are unlikely to look favorably upon whoever is in power at that time. I am hoping for a peaceful transition where those in power willingly acknowledge their shortcomings, follow the plan of dissolution and liquidation outlined in this book, and respectfully request mercy and forgiveness from the population. I do not know to what degree the population will show it to them, but they surely have a better chance of receiving forgiveness if they do this willingly, rather than standing to the end in their attempts to oppress and control society.

Either way, the power will shift and ultimately, it will be up to the new holders of this power to decide what image they would like to form society in.

I support the existence of property rights and believe the vast majority of those who support freedom and own hard assets feel the same way. As such, I propose that in lieu of government sponsored security, a charitably-funded societal-wide security force should be formed, which I am dubbing the First Security Force of the Free World (FSFFW). I will be referring to this force throughout this book as it relates to various considerations. For a full list of the mandates I propose to govern the FSFFW, see the appendix.

The FSFFW will respond to incidents of theft, vandalism, looting, and trespassing, in addition to incidents of assault or imminent threats of such. This includes protection against both domestic and foreign nations or groups. While individuals will be free to own weapons and to form their own local militias, one group will inevitably become the biggest and strongest. Many individuals in our society are unarmed or have insufficient arms to protect themselves from more numerous armed opponents. By instilling a single society-wide security force, we can avoid a society of feuding warlords, along with the inevitable racketeering that may happen in the absence of a centralized authority.

Regarding assault, there are some instances where the line needs to be clearly defined, including abortion and incidents of sex with a minor. Different people disagree on what should be the proper age of consent, and they also disagree on at what stage of development a fetus becomes a human being. My proposal for both situations is that we determine the cut-off through a democratic vote of those who willfully donate their wealth to support the FSFFW. For each dollar (new gold dollar, not old fiat dollar) a person contributes, they get to vote on what the age of consent should be. Out of all votes received, we will take the median vote as the one that will determine the age of consent. Whatever that age is, the FSFFW will seek to prevent sexual activity occurring with people under that age. Likewise, those who contribute dollars to the FSFFW will vote on what age they believe a fetus becomes a human being and the FSFFW will seek to prevent abortions occurring before that age. Keep in mind that if

27

the bulk of people donating to the FSFFW are strictly pro-life, the median age may be conception, meaning that the FSFFW would seek to prevent all abortions.

The FSFFW should have the mandates it has (for the proposed list, see Appendix) and no others, and we should consider the implications of that. If someone breaks a contract and another person seeks to violently harm the individual breaking the contract, the FSFFW will come to the defense of the individual being violently threatened. This means that slavery will be unacceptable in this society. If someone uses slave labor prevents the slaves from escaping under threat of violence, this will be a problem that will be dealt with by the FSFFW.

Understandably, there are some critical roles in society and a person walking off such a job might create some major problems. For this reason, it will be very important for companies to consider the reputations of those individuals they hire for critical positions, and to consider a contingent plan for the event they walk off the job.

Likewise, a person who loans money to someone else and doesn't get paid back will also be protected from violence by the FSFFW. For this reason, creditors will need to use discretion in determining who to lend to.

A person who defaults on a debt or walks away from a contracted agreement will likely gain a poor reputation in the community. Reputation will be a critical thing for people to maintain in this new economy, as will be discussed throughout this book, and this reality will be discovered by individuals as they experience life in our new and free society.

Aside from the situation where a person is being confined on someone else's land, the FSFFW will assume the land owner is the victim in other cases of violent confrontation. If a person is violent when people visit their land, there is no reason anyone should be visiting their land and they should leave as soon as possible. It will be up to those in our society who have compassion for them to welcome them into their homes or to support shelters that may house them.

It may be that some individuals choose to accept a certain amount of violence in exchange for the benefits provided by the owner of the land. Perhaps a child will put up with a parent's spanking if they feel it was the disciplinary aspect of an overall loving approach, or perhaps someone's domestic partner or spouse will feel the same way the first few times they get slapped in the face. As long as no one is being restricted from leaving by a landowner, the FSFFW will not seek to prevent the violence of the landowner, but will instead seek to protect that landowner from unwanted trespassers.

In a situation where two people own land jointly and there is a physical confrontation between the owners in which the FSFFW has been called, the FSFFW will seek to curtail the violence and then speak with both parties to attempt to find a peaceful resolution. Perhaps they can mediate a buy-out of one of the owners, perhaps the parties can promise not to be violent with each other anymore, or perhaps they will determine they must sell the property. If one party wishes to sell their interest in the property, they will be enabled to do so and protected by the FSFFW from violence in retaliation for any broken contract. The only consequence they should face for such a broken contract will be a potential loss of their reputation in the community.

Another question with relation to the FSFFW is the treatment of animals. Clearly if someone is abusing another person's animal, that is a violation of a property right and the FSFFW can step in to protect that property. But what if someone is abusing an animal that they themselves own?

Different people will disagree as to what constitutes animal abuse. Some will say abuse is limited to domestic animals while some will consider raising animals for meat to be abuse. The way to resolve this, like the abortion and age of consent issues, should be through contribution-based vote. Those supporting the FSFFW should determine whether the force will protect animals and the vote will allow them to do this. Their ballots will ask them whether various classes of animals should be protected and for the animal classes they vote yes on, the FSFFW will step in to

29

protect those classes of animals. So, perhaps the voters vote to protect domestic dogs and cats but not cattle being raised for meat. A new election can be held annually to determine if the desires of the voting population have changed.

As society becomes more prosperous under the free-market conditions outlined in this book, the morality of society is likely to advance as people gain more market power to demand others behave ethically and launch boycotts against those who don't. Over time, things that are acceptable in the early days may become unacceptable later. If most people are relying on cheap meat for food, it's likely they will vote not to have the FSFFW protect these animals but once people can pay the additional cost to eat animals raised in a more ethical manner, they will be more likely to vote to protect animals to a greater extent.

The FSFFW should not act to enforce any rules beyond those stated in this section. While different people will disagree on the morality of various activities including drinking alcohol, smoking cigarettes, using street drugs, gambling, and prostitution, the differences in morals regarding these topics are great and it would be exceedingly difficult to create a force powerful enough to be the dominant force in society through voluntary contributions alone if it was engaged to enforce such measures. Furthermore, there's a good chance they would fund their own army to contest for power. By having a single dominant security force that allows each landowner to set their own moral rules, we can provide people with individual freedom while allowing market forces to punish or reward landowners based on the popularity of their rules amongst their employees, customers, and other relationships.

We are a diverse society from a moral standpoint. In the later section on zoning, I will discuss how communities can form with local rules against behaviors without requiring societal-wide enforcement, providing people with the opportunity to physically isolate themselves from behaviors they find personally repugnant. In the section on regulations, I will discuss how economic pressure can be used to dissuade behavior that people see as immoral without requiring the use of physical force. Using force to enforce morality beyond the essential requirements of keeping people and their property physically safe will not be effective in changing the minds of those who hold a different morality and will only be effective in driving divisions between people and inspiring conflict. If we believe others are behaving immorally and we wish them to adjust their behavior, it is up to us to make our arguments using words, and not the barrel of a gun.

Justice

If the FSFFW shows up and stops an armed robber, there will need to be a mechanism in place to make sure the incident does not reoccur. If the armed robber is killed in a shootout with the FSFFW, the problem is resolved, but what if they surrender peacefully?

When this occurs, the perpetrator of the crime should be taken into custody by the FSFFW. First, the perpetrator(s) and victim(s) should be consulted to see if they can find a mutually agreeable resolution to their dispute. If not, each party will be given an opportunity to provide their viewpoint, along with the viewpoints of any witnesses they call, in a recording that will be uploaded to a website where the voting contributors of the FSFFW will determine their fate through a democratic process. Potentially punishments can include death, exile from the free world, or imprisonment.

It will likely be inefficient for all FSFFW members to vote on all cases that occur so some may decide to allow a third party to vote on cases on their behalf based upon their personal morality. There will likely be multiple third parties who do this that each represent a different set of values.

You may notice that each situation where the FSFFW will vote on an outcome is one where people with different morals are likely to vote differently. The morality perceptions of society evolve over time and by having a voting mechanism, this evolution will be reflected in the actions of the FSFFW. Prior to the formation of this FSFFW, discussion can be had about its rules but once it is formed, that discussion is over. If people later determine they would prefer to support a competing organization with a different set of rules, it will be up to them to charitably fund that cause. For this reason, I have referred to it as the "First" Security Force of the Free World.

While the FSFFW will administer justice regarding those caught in the act of a crime, it will not seek to resolve crimes that have already occurred by enacting justice on behalf of those

32

victims. If people want justice in such situations, they will need to take matters into their own hands and if that justice is violent, they will need to seek to escape the notice of the FSFFW.

There are certain organizations in America that have a history and reputation of administering violence. It is highly likely that such organizations may market a sort of "justice insurance" policy to people where they agree they will impart violence on behalf of those individuals who have done certain types of damage against them. If these organizations are smart, they will make instances of their imparting justice well-known to the public to dissuade people from acting in egregious ways against those who have one of their justice insurance policies, thereby minimizing the number of claims they must administer. Through doing so, they can improve their bottom line.

Some individuals may choose to display the name of their justice insurance company on their front door to dissuade potential assailants from entering. Others may choose to remain anonymous but with an unknown number of justice and security industry participants, there will soon materialize a high risk to anyone who seeks to treat others with violence. People will soon discover violence is a poor method of doing business in a free society and that there are better methods of satisfying one's desires.

While the FSFFW will respond to incidents where a person is actively under threat, it won't seek to stop an organization that offers to administer justice for others, recognizing that doing so falls outside of its own mandates. While a justice insurance company would need to use discretion to disburse said justice without drawing the attention of the FSFFW, if they can get away from the scene of the crime, they will not have to answer to the FSFFW, only to other parties who may potentially want to extract justice in retribution against them.

We need to have a discourse with the most violent offenders in our society to understand the reasons for their behavior and to see if there are ways their behavior can be adjusted so they may integrate into a peaceful society. There are many reasons violence has occurred in our society including economic desperation, struggles for political power and occasional sadism. Free markets will provide people with nonviolent economic opportunities and there will be no struggles for political power when there is no political body ruling over the country.

With a free market in entertainment, voluntary masochists can allow sadists to injure them in ways that are voluntarily agreed to in a controlled environment in exchange for a fee. While such perversions may seem disturbing to you or me, I cannot judge that which gives others satisfaction and to the degree that such supply and demand can be linked up in a way that directs these impulses against the willing rather than the innocent, we may avoid some of the great tragedies that occur when these impulses remain unexpressed and unfulfilled.

Despite that one potentially helpful solution, there are individuals in this society who have already committed great acts of violence against others and in the absence of the state's justice, it is likely many of these individuals will be hunted down and killed by those who will seek to impart their own form of justice against them. For violent offenders, it is important to attempt either a direct or indirect discourse between the offenders and those who cared for the victims. The state's involvement in such cases needs to end, the prisons need to be emptied to the greatest extent possible and the buildings formerly used as prisons need to be sold to raise money for the population.

The question of whether the prisoners should be executed, be exiled, remain imprisoned or be forgiven needs to be resolved by those involved with the case. The governments releasing prisoners will need to retain the services of those willing and capable of mediating between the victims and offenders to determine agreements that are mutually agreeable. Such an agreement may end up being something like "you take the lethal injection now and are spared what we would do to you if they let you go, and we get to know you are not out there on the streets threatening others."

34

In situations where it seems no assurance could be provided to society that the individual could ever be safe on the loose, the prisoners will either need to be executed or remain imprisoned. Because governments will have no funds to run prisons following the economic collapse, they will need to contract with private charities set up to keep these individuals imprisoned.

While the FSFFW will generally act to prevent groups outside of itself from imprisoning others, it will make an exception for legacy prisoners of the old system who have committed violent crimes great enough that they are deemed a continued threat to society. Private charities may administer such prisons for as long as it is necessary to do so, but there will be some conditions.

Upon the formation of the FSFFW, those who contribute to its funding will vote on what percentage of the old prison system prisoners should be deemed too violent to release. If the voted percentage is 20 percent and a particular state prison system has 1,000 prisoners, 800 of those prisoners will be released to meet the mandate.

The FSFFW will also monitor the activities of the new charitably funded prisons. Each prison will be evaluated independently and voting FSFFW contributors will periodically vote on whether they consider that prison to be humane. If greater than 50 percent of the votes consider it to be inhumane, the FSFFW will seek to liberate the prisoners of that prison by improving the conditions or moving them to a more humane facility.

No prisoner should be sentenced to the new charitably funded prisons other than the violent offenders transitioning from the legacy system and any new prisoners sentenced to imprisonment through vote of the FSFFW contributors for crimes with a person caught red-handed. If people seek imprisonment as a method of justice outside of those constraints, they will have a difficult time getting it, for the FSFFW will seek to prevent any such facilities from operating. Those seeking to extract justice for other crimes will need to use more creative methods of punishment that don't require operating a long-term facility that may be discovered by the FSFFW.

Agriculture

Food is one of the most basic demands in an economy, and all humans demand it. It is necessary for our survival and the percentage of the population that survives our transition to freedom will largely depend on how efficiently we are able to plant, grow, harvest, ship, produce, process, package and deliver food to the population.

Many in our society have recently become concerned about supply chain shortages but what we have experienced up to this point is nothing compared to what we are likely to experience from now until the time government steps out of the way and grants us our freedom. Supply chains do not just grow themselves overnight but are an agglomeration of countless businesses that have grown up over time, and this process has been going on throughout human history. We have never experienced an economic reset to the extent of the one that we are about to face and the only chance we will have to survive will be complete economic freedom.

With relation to agriculture, that means anyone who owns land should be free to grow and sell anything they want on that land[2]. Some may be concerned that people will produce products that are unsafe, but such concerns are unfounded. Each producer of food will develop their own reputation and each consumer will decide what risks they are willing to assume to purchase and consume a product. Consumers will need to evaluate the risks they are assuming if consuming products of producers who lack a good reputation of producing safe products. But if a starving person has a choice between eating food that has a ten percent chance of making them sick or not eating any food, it is kinder to offer them the ninety percent chance of a good meal than no chance whatsoever.

---

[2] This excludes people living within certain local zones and HOAs that have rules against it. These circumstances will be discussed in the zoning section

Food producers will quickly gain a reputation amongst their potential customers. If they are producing bad products, people will stop buying from them and instead buy from their competitors. It is likely a demand will materialize for food inspection and the companies that inspect it will then develop their own reputations. Those who can provide good inspections at the lowest cost are likely to win market share and consumers will start relying on these companies to tell them which products are safe to eat.

Freedom is essential because as much of the supply chain as has been disrupted through government's action up until now, an even larger part will be disrupted when government becomes unable to pay for its expenditures and companies need to find new suppliers and distributors for their business. It is tragic to see a crop die in a farmer's field because no one arrived to deliver it somewhere. In a free economy, people would be free to take their trucks to such locations to take away some of that crop and deliver it to someone who could use it, paying a bargain-basement price to take it off the farmer's hands and at least allowing the farm to recoup some of its investment. This food could then be delivered to food processors or even sold as a raw ingredient in farmers' markets to whoever in that market demands that item. Without government hoops to jump through, anyone with the means to physically move products and the capital to purchase them could get involved with the process, connecting supply with demand, reducing waste, and assisting in the population's struggle against starvation.

The United States has a lot of good potential farmlands, even though many of them have been unused in recent years due to various government programs that discourage production. A free market in agriculture can transform this barren land into productive land and create the food products that will be so desperately needed in the United States, and around the world, in the wake of this collapse. We can produce whatever crops yield the most return on investment, provide jobs for some of the millions of people who will find themselves with little hope in the wake of this financial collapse, and start to build the base level of an economy that will someday dwarf anything this world has seen.

Utilities

Perhaps even more critical than food production is access to clean drinking water. A person can potentially survive for months without food but without clean water, a person will perish within a few days.

Fortunately, most utility companies in the United States have been operating on a for-profit model where people have had to pay for services such as water, gas, electricity, and trash collection. The utility companies or governments that have been administering these services will need to start pricing their services in a new currency whereby their customers can transfer value to them in exchange for the service. This will likely be the new gold dollar, but they may also start accepting alternative currencies if they expect this will allow them to facilitate additional sales.

Government-operated utilities will need to decide how to best move forward while minimizing hardships to their community. It might make sense for the government to temporarily continue operating the utility for some period, acting as an essentially private company funded entirely by its sale of services. Any profits would be contributed to that government's pool of assets available for disbursement to its population. Later, the utility could be sold to a private party while the government's proceeds on the sale could also then be distributed to the population.

Some states may decide to allocate a portion of their disbursement of the gold reserve towards the temporary continued operation of some of these services to allow populations to prepare for the day they end, or to allow time for the government or purchasing private party to determine how to make the venture profitable.

In other instances, it may make the most sense for the government venture to be immediately sold to a private company that will then begin operating the utility for profit. Many government services haven't been raising enough revenue to cover their costs and have therefore relied on tax dollars to make up the difference. But even though the government may not be able to operate the venture profitably, a private company might be able to do so by acquiring the government's assets and making the necessary structural changes to the operation.

Another option is for the assets of the utility to be sold to a newly charitably funded organization that will have the objective of providing that utility to as many people as possible in that community based on the private donations it receives. If there are insufficient donations up front for the charity to purchase the assets from the government, and the management of the charity has a good reputation, the government could consider extending credit to the charity where they will be paid back over a period of years based on the donations the charity receives in the future. The government would accept the risk of losing the value of those assets but do so based on a positive expected return on their loan, as well as for the sake of providing their community with continuity in their utility services.

Perhaps the charity will only end up raising enough money for the community to have their lights on for two hours per day after paying back the government's loan, but that two hours will provide a great value for the community that they wouldn't otherwise have. As economic freedom provides additional economic opportunities for people in the community, the standard of living will increase and people will have more funds to donate to the causes they are about, such as funding public utilities.

Many utility companies will likely have a tiered model. Under such a model, someone willing and able to pay for electrical use could use as much as they want if they pay for it. Those unable or unwilling to pay would be relegated to just that couple of hours a day of electrical usage until their own prosperity, or the prosperity of the community they live in, has increased to a level where someone can pay for their additional usage.

41

Utility companies will have to come to terms with the reality that in the absence of government regulations, other service providers will be free to compete with them. Additionally, many individuals are likely to decide to migrate in the wake of our economic collapse in search of new economic opportunities. A booming agriculture market is likely to draw many people away from large cities and the government and government-related jobs that no longer exist there, and into the country. Many towns and cities are likely to become mostly or completely abandoned as their populations leave in search of economic opportunities.

Many utility companies may discover they no longer can provide the services they formerly provided to their community due to a lack of profitability, and that they need to liquidate their assets. By allowing markets to be free, market participants can buy up the assets of these failed ventures and put them to productive use. In the wake of all financial debts having been reset, companies will at least have the value of their physical assets and selling those assets can provide the owners with at least some amount of capital to put towards their next venture, whether it be in utilities or one of the many other industries that will boom once we have freedom.

Zoning

The greatest divide in our society in recent times has been between the pro-vaccine-mandate crowd and the anti-vaccine-mandate crowd. This specific issue seems to be the line in the sand across which the feuding human population have been throwing insults, threats, and other dubious items at one another for the past many months.

Each landowner should be free to set the rules for their own land in a free society. When I say they should be free, what I mean is that no one should, through force or threat of force, go onto someone else's land and tell them how to go about their business. The purpose of the FSFFW will be to ensure this outcome is enabled.

There are some situations where we need to determine who the rightful owner is and therefore, whose claim the FSFFW should be protecting. The rule that will result in the greatest continuity and peace will be for the legal owner under the former jurisdiction to continue as the legal and rightful owner moving forward.

Ownership does not refer to possession, but control. In the case of a landlord and a tenant, the landlord is the owner, even though the tenant has temporary possession. An employee may temporarily possess company-owned equipment for the purposes of fulfilling their job duties, but the company retains ownership of the equipment.

By viewing ownership from this perspective, we can see that in certain situations, an individual has not been a pure owner, but has shared ownership authority with other parties, most frequently the government. An individual may have had a certain amount of freedom to control what should be done with the land they have owned, but only within the parameters permitted by the government. When I suggest the former legal owner continue as the new owner, I am suggesting an increase in that owner's authority, because I am also suggesting a removal of government authority.

Their control will still not be absolute because the FSFFW will respond to calls of slavery or unauthorized handling of nuclear material even if it is taking place on a private party's land and that private party was not the one to make the call. But assuming people are not violating these basic rules, the FSFFW will not interfere with the private control of land, only showing up if the owner or tenant of the land requests assistance in protecting it from theft, vandalism, trespassing or invasion.

Additionally, the owner's authority may be limited based on the zoning laws that previously existed regarding the land or its inclusion in a homeowner's association. When individuals purchased property that was in a zone declared to be residential, industrial, or commercial by the ruling authority, they had the expectation that such zoning laws would continue, and a reasonable expectation that someone would not be opening a sewage plant in their neighborhood. Each area of land that was zoned for specific use by government will therefore need to elect its own leadership that will determine whether those zoning rules should continue.

The city government should not be involved in this process, other than to offer information related to the current zoning rules in existence and possibly to facilitate elections of zone leadership for zones that exist within its former jurisdiction. But the leadership of each zone should be elected by the landowners within that land. The landowners should determine which zoning rules will remain in effect for that area of land through a democratic process, either by electing a leader or council to make the determination, or by voting directly on which zoning provisions should continue.

While a democratic process can be used to determine which zoning rules should remain, no new zoning laws or rules should be added to except by unanimous consent of the landowners in that area, and the FSFFW will enforce this. A private property owner signed up for the zoning rules of a particular area when they purchased that property, but they should not be subjected to additional rules they did not sign up for. If people are interested in living somewhere with additional rules, they will need to either convince everyone in the location that the new proposed rules are desirable or move to a new location with other like-minded people.

Homeowner's associations are already set up as private organizations and so the transition of these should be smoother. If the homeowner's association can set new rules under the current regime, that's something the homeowners signed up for when they decided to purchase the property.

Communities that contain like-minded individuals as adjacent landowners may decide they want to form a new landowner's association, and to set rules that apply to all landowners in that community. Perhaps they will set rules that are unanimously agreed to by the owners such as no alcohol, no drugs, no prostitution, no gambling, or no entry without vaccination. They can set whatever local rules they want so long as they have the unanimous consent of those in their community.

In the utilities section, I referred to migration taking place due to people looking for economic opportunities, but it will also take place due to the vast cultural differences that exist between different groups of people. Without government determining what moral rules should be followed by the entirety society, each landowner will be free to set the rules for their own property, or to voluntarily join a community of like-minded landowners who will follow a given set of rules on the land they collectively own. Many individuals living in locations where their personal moral beliefs are a minority viewpoint may find that they would be more comfortable migrating to a location that better reflects their own morality.

By allowing each individual and each business to decide what rules are best for the property they own, it is likely that many communities will sprout up with diverse cultures from each other, ultimately creating an interesting world of unique individuals and places to visit.

To an extent, this process is already occurring in our current society as different locations have set different COVID-related restrictions. By government getting out of the way and allowing economic markets to restructure, this process will continue and become more efficient, ultimately creating a world where there's somewhere for everyone.

Manufacturing

Once we have some of our most basic needs met through the development of free market security, justice, finance, agriculture, and utilities, it's time to start building things. While humans may survive for a long time off just food and clean water, the demands humans have beyond those essentials are great. People demand all types of other products including automobiles, appliances, furniture, clothing, medicines, hygiene items, electronics, jewelry, and toys. The list of human demands is endless and with a free market economy, investors can deploy their capital to begin the processes of growing, mining, refining, transporting, constructing, packaging, and delivering these products to their ultimate consumers.

Many of the processes required to produce these products are labor-intensive and in the absence of government restrictions, entrepreneurs will be enabled to set up and construct the facilities required to produce these products, drawing from the pool of available labor in the local region where the facilities are located.

For many years, Americans have lived above their means in the sense that our country has consumed more than it has produced, as evidenced by consistent trade deficits. People in places like China, Vietnam and other major manufacturing nations have worked hard to produce goods that have then been shipped across the world to America and consumed by Americans in exchange for debt, payable in United States dollars[3].

With the collapse of this credit bubble, Americans will no longer get such a sweet deal. Foreigners will no longer be willing to exchange their productive efforts for our debt, and our ability to consume will be solely a function of our own production.

When two nations trade with each other, doing so benefits both nations, just as trades between two individuals benefit both

---

[3] This will be discussed from the perspective of foreigners in the foreign nations section.

individuals. The reason is that a person will not engage in a trade unless they perceive the value of what they are receiving to be greater than the value of what they are giving up. Value is subjective to everyone, and it is this difference in subjective value that allows win-win trades to occur.

The more potential trading partners an individual or other entity has, the more opportunities it has to make beneficial trades and the better off it will ultimately be. For this reason, the US government should immediately cease any trading restrictions with foreign nations. Individuals and companies should also be hesitant to enact such restrictions personally. While a boycott can be an effective mechanism for social change, a topic that will be discussed in the later section on regulations, participating in one does entail an economic cost.

Existing in a global economy means producers have competitors from all over the world, including in locations with few labor laws. If someone wants to operate a successful manufacturing business, they will need to be able to produce products for less cost than their global price. If their competitor in Vietnam is paying a low wage with a slim profit margin, they will either need to match that low wage or find other ways to cut costs.

Ending government regulations and taxes will do a tremendous amount to make American businesses competitive and lower their costs, enabling them to pay higher amounts for labor. But the reality is, we will be living in a society with millions of unemployed and unskilled laborers desperate for work. It is likely that at first, the wage for unskilled labor will be low, in the sense of the standard of living it will provide for that laborer and their family.

Despite this, a free market will be the only chance we have to restore a healthy economy to our country and for most people, it will be the only chance they have of survival. Times will be tough for a while but if we have freedom, the hard work we do today will pay dividends in the future. The more factories that are opened, the more products will be produced and available for consumption with the wages being earned by the workers. As people work for longer, they will develop familiarity with their job duties and gain skills that are in demand, increasing the market value of their labor and the wages they can demand.

It has been a long time since manufacturing boomed in America and many of our formerly productive facilities are in disrepair or have been razed completely to make way for the residential and commercial construction that has been made possible with our credit bubble. There will be a great demand for construction workers as old productive facilities are restored to a state of operation and new facilities are built. Those in our society who already have construction skills will be greatly sought after to head up construction teams and teach those skills to the new generation of laborers who will be showing up on work sites.

Once the productive facilities are built, those who have survived up until this point can find new opportunities working in factories and receiving a paycheck where government withholds nothing. They can start using those checks to feed themselves, clothe themselves, house themselves and purchase some of the wide variety of products that will be available on the free market. They can deposit their savings in a bank that they trust, they can choose to invest their savings in new ventures that will provide them with passive income streams, or they can donate their wealth to a charitable cause that they personally feel compelled towards supporting. What they earn will be theirs to direct as they wish and as their skills increase, so will both their earnings and the number of things a person can buy with those earnings as we experience an economy with the wheels of production in full motion.

Transportation

"What about the roads?" I was asked, as if this single question refuted the idea that we don't need government. Being a kind person, I wrote a lengthy couple-page response that was aptly ignored by the asker of the question. It seems that individual wasn't really interested in listening to what I had to say, and that's why I'm writing this book.

I have engaged in countless interactions with people from across the spectrum of political and philosophical ideologies over the past few years. This book is entitled "human discourse" because it was my original intention to write a book suggesting that the solution to all human problems is an honest discourse between humans. While I still believe this, as you will read about in the love section, this is not a book about that idea. This is a book about the solutions that I have developed because of the discourse I've already been engaged in.

I am writing this book partially because I am tired of engaging in the same tired discourse over and over. The solutions to our problems are complex, requiring both creativity and an acknowledgement of reality. In a sense, any brief dialogue about a single issue or economic market is incomplete without the context of this entire book. It is not a book about one topic or one concern, but a comprehensive solution that I only want to have to write once. Once I have done that and published it in a book, all I have left to do is distribute that book. That sounds a lot better than engaging in repetitive and fruitless interactions with closed-minded people who only ask me questions to then ignore my answer and waste my time.

With all that said, the roads we have aren't going to just disappear overnight. They will remain here tomorrow, regardless of whether the government itself exists. The question is not who will build the roads, but who will maintain them, for they are already built. And with that, we can all take a deep breath.

The maintenance of the roads isn't an urgent issue in the sense of the rest of the topics discussed thus far in this book. Up until now, it's been about survival. It's been about how are we going survive the collapse of our economy to transition to a free society in a peaceful manner with the greatest societal continuity and while setting ourselves up for survival in the future. Now, we're discussing roads, things that exist today and will exist two weeks from now, regardless of what government does or does not do.

Roads are just one part of an overall transportation market that also includes bicycles, trains, ships, and aircraft. Without any government red tape to jump through, anyone can offer transportation services to the public and just as with buildings, each landowner or business can set its own rules. If an airline wants to allow smoking and carrying firearms during a flight, it will be free to do so. If another airline wants to model its business after the current system of T.S.A. pat-downs and mandatory masks, it will also be free to do so. If an airport wants to exclude aircraft that don't meet certain safety conditions to maintain its own reputation, it will be free to do so. If another airport has less strict regulations and wants to allow higher risk flights for a lower cost, it will also be free to do so.

The one area where some coordination will need to remain is with air-traffic control, for different airlines and airports need to coordinate with one another to prevent mid-air collisions. Like the FSFFW, air traffic control is an area where a centralized system makes sense. It won't end well if we have multiple air traffic control companies unaware of the flights other companies are monitoring.

The centralization of a market does not mean the population should be taxed to support that market. Those who fund the existence of a centralized air traffic control authority should be those who use it.

This is a rare circumstance where I will support a monopoly authority charging a fee in exchange for the service they provide. I am okay with their charging a fee based on flight miles because I don't foresee enough people or companies voluntarily donating to provide sufficient air traffic control, and it's a vital function that needs to take place with the complex grid of flights that take place in the modern world. Individuals or companies who fly without registering their flights with the centralized authority will be a hazard to society and the FSFFW should seek to keep them grounded.

There needs to be a mechanism in place to prevent this authority from abusing the monopoly it will have. It seems that the best way to align the interests of the potentially abused (those flying planes) and the potential abuser (the centralized air traffic control authority) is to have those who use the authority get to vote on who should head up the authority based on their flight miles and thus, the money they've paid to the authority.

The centralized air traffic control authority should have no ability to perform any functions other than air traffic control. It will not be up to this authority to deny flights from taking place based on aircraft safety, social issues, or other metrics. Anyone willing to pay the per-mile fee and able to get an aircraft into the air should be free to fly, so long as they respect the authority of the air traffic control authority for the purpose of avoiding collisions.

Roads are owned by all levels of government within the United States and each government will have to determine how to dispose of their roads. Some may decide to keep them in their possession for a period and rely on charitable contributions from the community to maintain them. Others may decide to sell their roads to private owners, either as an outright sale of the land with all rights attached, or as a conditional sale where the new owner must agree to keep the property as a road available for private use for some number of years. The conditions of the sale can be made very specific including the tolls or advertising that the new owner can collect or display on the new road. Each government should consider the transportation needs of its population, the offers it has available, and how to maximize its liquidation proceeds. The only constraint is that they may not collect future tax dollars to fund road maintenance.

It is likely that once we have freedom, the transportation demands of society will shift dramatically. Many formerly bustling cities will have little activity and their freeways will be abandoned as the government and government-related jobs that once existed in those cities no longer do. Roads in such places will have diminished need for maintenance, while other locations will demand new roads.

Whenever there is an unmet demand in society, there is an opportunity for someone to fill it. In the absence of government restrictions, entrepreneurs can get creative in the transportation options they offer. Privately owned buses can transport people from A to B while private roads can be funded through either tolls, roadside advertising or charitable contributions made by local individuals and businesses.

The roads we've been driving on have been maintained by governments that have maintained a host of traffic laws including rules for stopping at red lights and stop signs, driving below the speed limit, and abstaining from drinking and driving.

The FSFFW will not be enforcing these rules so it will be up to each road owner to set and enforce their own policies, and each road user to use the requisite discretion in the decisions they make. Transportation consumers will be faced with trade-offs in many circumstances: higher risk and lower cost, or lower risk but higher cost. Like with airlines, different market participants can have different policies and cater to different customers with different priorities.

It is likely that road servicing organizations will spring up and outsource their services to road owners. That way, one organization can maintain the traffic lights and dui checkpoints for multiple road owners in a region.

Yes, we can still expect there will be DUI checkpoints, even though there is no government and even though the FSFFW will not be enforcing drunk driving rules. Each road owner will set their own policies and if the road's consumers demand that people don't drive drunk on the road they're using, they can hire officers to pull people over and fine those who are driving drunk or violating other traffic laws. If the fine is not paid, they can be excluded from using that road and their name can be entered in a directory of bad road customers that other road owners may also want to exclude. If someone attempts to use the road after being excluded, they will have crossed the threshold into trespassing and at the request of the road's owner, the FSFFW will get involved.

Like the centralized air traffic authority, ocean harbors previously managed by the government may need a centralized authority to determine which ships may enter and leave the harbor and to avoid shipwrecks. Like the air traffic authority, the fees for the harbor authority should be paid by the ship owners using the harbor, and the management of that authority should be voted on based on harbor usage and thus, money paid in. The harbor authority should not be inspecting ships or their contents, serving only to direct ships in and out.

The transportation industry is a massive one and there is great complexity in the network that is in place. The importance of each service formerly provided by government needs to be considered, and a plan needs to be undertaken to transition that service to the private sector, for government will have no further ability to collect tax dollars to pay for its endeavors. I am not an expert in the industry and there will surely be other issues and complexities that arise as the process of privatization is undertaken. What I am confident of is that human discourse can build us a bridge to wherever we want to go.

Healthcare

I don't trust Big Pharma and I have no intention to take a COVID vaccine. I don't need to discuss my reasons because they are irrelevant to the topic at hand, and I have no expectation that anyone would be convinced one way or another by my feelings on the topic. The topic at hand is freedom and it is the solution for all our healthcare concerns.

It doesn't matter whether you support vaccinations or vaccine mandates because in a free society, you could visit the establishments and communities that have rules you agree with. You could keep to your own and I could keep to mine. People could mind their own business and stop acting like nags and tyrants in attempting to conform the entire society to their personal vision of morality.

The FSFFW won't be going after neglectful behavior (see previous section on drunk driving) but remain focused on direct threats to people and their property. As such, the FSFFW won't be interested in whether a manufacturer is producing an unsafe vaccine or whether individuals in society are failing to keep others as safe as possible by taking a vaccine. Market regulation will be distinct from security and will be discussed in a later section.

Freedom in medicine and healthcare means there will be no more patent protection for the development of medications. In fact, there will be no intellectual property laws at all. The FSFFW will protect against the theft of physical property, but it is up to each individual or company to safeguard its own intellectual property to the best of its ability.

In many circumstances, this will be impossible. A pill can be easily examined, and its ingredients determined, enabling competitors to produce the same substance. Fairly immediately, many medications that have previously been either under patent, difficult to get a prescription for, or outright illegal will become available at a low cost to the population.

While we have previously relied on pharmaceutical companies to do the necessary research to develop new medications, such companies don't need to be the ones funding or conducting such research. Individuals interested in fighting disease and healing people can donate to charities that research and develop new medicines. Without a profit motive, such research can be pure and focused on health, rather than on how to patent a substance for profit[4].

The government's involvement in our healthcare and education system has resulted in a single-minded approach to medicine and the Covid experience has shown us that those who question that single-minded approach in our current society have typically been threatened with losses of funding, licensing, and credibility. This is a flawed approach to any field of intellectual inquiry and by removing government licensing and funding from the picture, a truly competitive market can arise.

Sages throughout the world have spoken of natural cures and alternative approaches to medicine, but this wisdom has been largely neglected or ignored in the West. By allowing anyone to practice medicine, new alternatives will hit the marketplace and people will have a better chance of finding care that heals them while also respecting their spiritual and ethical principles and beliefs.

Those who favor the legacy medical system can continue to access such care if they can afford to. Without government checks going out to healthcare providers and customers, it is likely we will see a crash in healthcare prices, and a widely diminished interest in people spending their hard-earned money on such care.

Many of the older generation have relied on Medicare, a program that will be a casualty of the coming economic collapse. Without that option, it is likely that many older people will be forced to survive for as long as they can outside of the healthcare system. Hopefully, there are people in their families and communities who can step up to help support them through their

---

[4] This same principle applies to other intellectual property and will be discussed in the technology section.

final days on this planet. The baby boomer generation has lived to see the rise of the largest credit bubble in history and will likely be shocked to see the collapse of that bubble. Many of these individuals have worked hard for their entire lives, despite the reality that many of those efforts will ultimately end in futility. It will be a great kindness if those of us still able to earn choose to contribute to their continued survival.

Education

For some reason, society has decided it's a good idea to have all our children attend similar schools and learn a similar curriculum through their formulative years. It's not.

Every individual on our planet is unique, and every child is unique. Different people have different interests and different aptitudes. While there are some basic skills such as reading, writing and arithmetic that almost everyone in our society can benefit from, the extent to which each individual needs to master each of these fields, and others, is different.

Diversity in knowledge and skills is beneficial to society because when society consists of people with differing abilities, people can specialize in those things towards which they are most inclined and produce that specific thing in great quantities before trading it with other people in society who also specialize.

Society benefits from specialization because a specialist can typically produce that which they specialize in more efficiently and effectively than a generalist could. Instead of having to use a single generalist to build my house, raise the crops I eat, give me dental care, and stitch my clothing, I can use different specialists for each of these functions, resulting in higher quality and more affordable products.

Upon the forthcoming economic collapse, governments will no longer be able to maintain their schools and so parents will have to determine who should watch their children while they work. While some families may choose to have a stay-at-home parent educate their children and some may pay to send them to private schools, many will have few economic means for either of those options.

In these circumstances, families will need to start making alternative arrangements. One idea that will likely be tried by many families is to rotate parents watching a large group of children. If ten families have twenty kids between them, one family can watch those kids every ten days. Without government schools, the traditional workweek will likely start to fade as a concept and many employers will be willing to schedule time off in ways that are agreeable to their employees.

By having a different parent teaching them each day in a ten-day rotation, the children will gain a more diverse education that they would have sitting in a government classroom while learning from a single adult presenting the government-approved curriculum.

A great demand for childcare will exist once government schools become unfunded and this will offer an economic opportunity for the older generation who can no longer do the physical labor other jobs will require. Because they have a lifetime of experience, they are ideal for the role of teaching children and preparing them for their lives to come.

Universities have been largely supported by government programs and the demand for a college education will collapse once the government is no longer able to finance the bill, and young adults no longer have the luxury of spending some of their prime physical years outside of the workforce. Many universities will need to liquidate large parts of their campuses, and some will likely shut their doors entirely. They will have to rely on tuition from those few students still priviledged enough to spend their prime years in such a place, as well as private donations.

Some colleges may decide to shift their curriculum to one that will better prepare people for the workforce. Trade schools that teach technical skills translatable to the working world will have an easier time selling education than liberal arts colleges. Just like other companies, each institution will have to decide for itself whether it still is a going concern, and whether its assets should be liquidated.

Regulation

Throughout this book, I have touched on the idea that markets will regulate themselves without assistance from government. In this section, I will expand upon that idea and discuss the specific mechanisms by which our economy can encourage safe products and socially responsible companies.

Just as I believe it has been an error for libertarians to appeal to socialists on moral grounds, I believe it is an error for society to demand responsible behavior from companies on moral grounds. As I mentioned in the morality section, different individuals have different ideas about what is moral. Just because I judge the behavior of someone else as immoral doesn't mean that individual cares about my judgement or will be inclined to change their behavior.

A far more effective tool of encouraging behavior is when a company's bottom line is rewarded by participating in ethical behavior or hurt for a failure to do so. Regardless of their moral beliefs, all companies care about their bottom line. Even if they only want to make money so they can donate it to a cause they believe in, they still want to make that money.

The money a company makes is largely determined by the number of people willing to be their customer, to work for them, or to otherwise be engaged in business with them. The willingness of people to fulfill these functions is based on the benefits they get from that relationship and how they feel about engaging in that relationship.

If a company is acting in ways that are seen as unethical by its consumers, those consumers will decide to shop with a different company, assuming a competitor exists who produces the same product at the same price but with a higher ethical standard. This economic pressure is the tool by which consumers can ultimately determine which companies are successful and which ones fail, due to their ethical practices.

Everything is a trade-off and consumers demanding higher ethical standards and safer products will likely have to pay for more expensive products. Quality has a price and consumers need to individually determine how much they are willing to pay to get it.

A free society will provide the maximum economic opportunities for individuals, and this will ultimately empower them to participate in boycotts as necessary to encourage socially responsible behavior from companies. There will be more companies seeking their labor, meaning they will have more negotiating power regarding their wages and working conditions. Earning more will allow them to pay more for products that meet their ethical demands. More companies will be producing products, making it easier for consumers to boycott a particular company and instead use its competitors' products.

In a free society, new businesses will arise to monitor individual and company reputations. Consumers can decide what conditions they want to set to purchase a company's products and businesses can decide what conditions they want to set to hire people. Likewise, businesses can decide if there are customers they do not wish to serve, and employees can decide which companies they want to work for.

Some may fear harsh outcomes from this, such as a business that openly discriminates based on an arbitrary factor such as race. But in today's social climate, such a business is likely to draw the attention of not only organizations such as Black Lives Matter that seek racial justice, but also from the general population who are not typically politically active but may become radicalized by such an egregious policy.

This would have a negative financial impact on the business in many ways. If there are protestors outside the business, they may have to hire extra security. Customers are likely not to visit the business, either because they disagree with the discriminatory policy or because they fear retribution from those who do. The media will be likely to cover the story and paint their business in a negative light that will be difficult to recover from. Ultimately, the business is likely to fail.

However, even if the business withstands all of this and enough racists come out of the woodwork to support them, what harm is truly being done? They can have their racist party and people who aren't interested in being associated with them can simply stay away from that business or community, choosing instead to associate themselves with those who do not discriminate.

While our current economy has included a certain amount of reputation reporting including credit agencies, investment rating agencies and the Better Business Bureau, a free market will likely offer additional reputation reporting options, allowing individuals and companies to determine which parties they are interested in doing business with. A person's reputation will become extremely important in a free society and markets will cater to the inevitable demand that people will have to know the reputation of those they are dealing with.

Many have supported government regulations to prevent companies from polluting. Some economists even refer to pollution as an externality, a transaction that provides a benefit to the polluting company while socializing the cost amongst everyone on our planet who suffers from a degraded environment. While it may be fair to see pollution in this light, centralized control over polluters is unnecessary.

The individuals living in the society ultimately will determine how much pollution they are willing to put up with in exchange for the products they consume. Those interested in ecological issues can seek to shed light on the polluting ways of offending companies and inspire boycotts of their products until they have reduced their ecological impact. Alternatively, they can personally contribute to causes such as reforestation that fight against humanity's destruction of the environment.

Both boycotts and charitable contributions will be enabled by having free economic markets where individual economic opportunities are maximized. The more prosperous society becomes, the more luxury people will have to participate in and contribute to the causes they care about, whether those causes are the ecology of our planet or something else.

Disasters

When disaster strikes, people have become accustomed to turning to government with their hands stretched out asking for assistance. With the collapse of the credit bubble, government will no longer be able to respond to disasters and people will need to prepare for their inevitability.

Fires can happen anywhere and without firefighters responding quickly, they can rage out of control and produce widespread destruction. In the absence of government, individuals will need to purchase fire protection for the buildings they own, and fire departments will need to sell such protection to fund themselves.

The market for fire protection is similar to the market for security in that a person is benefitted not only from personal protection, but from living in a community that is protected. It does little good to protect the company's headquarters from theft and violence if their employees' route to work, their customer's route to their retail outlets and their supply chain is not also protected. And just as it makes sense for people interested in living in a safe society to donate to the FSFFW, it also will likely make sense for people to contribute to a fire protection force that covers an area larger than simply their own property.

With both security and fire protection, we are faced with the reality of freeloaders who will accept the protection but not contribute to support it, favoring other causes instead. It is what it is. If people in the community are unwilling to contribute sufficient funds to these causes, then their communities will remain unprotected, and they will have to accept the risks that entails.

As with all potential causes, they will be better funded if the population is in a better financial position to do so, and freedom is what will provide the population with the opportunities to improve their financial positions. Without taxes, people will have their entire earned income at their disposal and contribute money towards those causes that they consider having the highest priority. For some, this may be communal fire protection and national security while for others, this may be orphanages and reforestation. Charitable giving will be discussed in greater detail in the charity section.

Fires are unique amongst disasters because of their ability to spread, making them a community problem more than other disasters that strike who they strike, but do not spread and threaten others after the original strike. For disasters such as hurricanes, tornadoes, floods, and earthquakes, it is up to property owners to purchase the requisite insurance policies to protect them from these disasters.

Any relief efforts typically performed by government will need to be performed by private charitable organizations if they are to be performed at all. Free markets can also help with relief efforts as without government red tape to deal with, people will be free to buy, move and sell products at whatever prices the market will bear. While governments frequently have responded to natural disasters by enacting price controls to prevent so-called price gouging, these policies are destructive and only lead to shortages.

[5]Imagine there is a water shortage following a natural disaster and the only seller of bottled water in an area has 100 bottles for sale. If he is allowed to sell them for $100 apiece, people will only buy that water for the most desperate purposes, such as for drinking water necessary to survive. If instead, a price gouging law is in effect and each bottle is being sold for $1, his first customer might arrive with $100 and decide to buy up the entire inventory so he can drink water, wash his dishes and clothes, and maybe even water his plants. Now, the second customer will arrive with a desperate need for drinking water and

---

[5] I recall Peter Schiff used this example of bottled water when discussing price gouging on one of his podcasts. While the same principles of supply and demand apply to all markets, Schiff's bottled water example is as good as any I can come up with to illustrate the problem of price gouging laws, and so I have used his example here which I hope he does not mind. For a link to Peter Schiff's YouTube channel, check out my website www.humandiscourse.com.

discover the proprietor has sold out of bottles. Prices reflect supply and demand and if the price is high, that is because it needs to be.

If someone in an adjacent area unaffected by the disaster catches wind that water bottles are selling for $100, he might load up his truck with water bottles and deliver them to the disaster area to make a profit for himself. While some may judge it as wrong to make a profit in a disaster area, it is not wrong if the purchasers of the water are better off for his delivering them. They are happy to pay the higher price because they need the water desperately. While it would be nice if the guy had delivered the bottles for free, we should not hold someone else accountable for being such a hero. Maybe he needed that money to feed his own family and would otherwise have needed to go to work and not have been able to afford the time, gas, and water to deliver to the disaster area. Regardless of his intentions, his behavior improves the situation in the disaster area, while the government policy would have prevented it. At the end of the day, it is more important to improve the situation on this planet than to criticize someone helping that situation for not helping more.

Nuclear Power

Humans have discovered an element named uranium that holds within it incredible power that we have been able to access. Through a process of enrichment, uranium found in the ground is transformed into a form of fuel capable of great good or great harm, depending on how it is used.

This uranium can either be harnessed into nuclear weapons or into nuclear power plants used to generate electricity. There is a fixed amount of uranium on our planet and once it has been used up, it can be used no more.

While I support an almost entirely free market in weaponry, I draw a line at nuclear weapons, due to their great ability to create widespread harm. As much damage as a psychotic individual can do with an automatic weapon, they could do manyfold more damage with a nuclear weapon. For this reason, I support the establishment of an international nuclear watchdog that will monitor the use of nuclear material by those possessing it.

As the nation owning the most nuclear weapons, it is the duty of the United States government to spearhead a multilateral nuclear disarmament agreement between nuclear nations. There is no reason any nuclear weapons should exist on this planet. Any that do should be dismantled with their fuel being repurposed for nuclear power plants if possible and destroyed if not.

Once this has happened, an international watchdog should be established that will monitor the owners of nuclear material to ensure it is tracked and not being used to create weapons. This organization should have the right to inspect the facilities of the holders of nuclear material for this purpose and should be funded through the voluntary contributions of those interested in preventing humans from engaging in nuclear conflict. Those who contribute should vote on the leadership of the organization with voting power based on how much they have contributed. Their findings should be available for all of humanity to see.

To the degree that other nations refuse to disarm or allow the international watchdog access to inspect its nuclear facilities, the watchdog should maintain an arsenal of its own nuclear weapons, inherited from the United States arsenal, to provide it with second strike capability in the event of a nuclear attack.

The watchdog to prevent nuclear war should be separate from any regulatory companies used by nuclear power companies and their customers to ensure safe plant operations. Those who choose to live near nuclear power plants should understand the risks involved and free market regulators and inspectors will surely spring up so that nuclear power companies can use their reports to reassure the local public of their safety.

In the fight against global warming, nuclear power plants can be a great boon due to their lack of greenhouse gas emissions. Our supply of oil, natural gas and coal is being continuously depleted and someday we will be unable to use these resources to power our cities. We will eventually have to rely almost exclusively on solar, wind and hydroelectric power for electricity but from now until that day, nuclear power can provide us with a safe, reliable, and clean energy source to reduce our current greenhouse gas emissions and buy us time until solar technology is up to speed.

Not only this, but the expansion of nuclear power plants will deplete the world of its supply of uranium. Perhaps someday, we will deplete it entirely and the threat of nuclear war will be one that is only read about in history books.

Entertainment

Once the basic infrastructure and production of society has been established, people will start looking for ways to occupy their free time. In the early days, most people will be working as much as their bodies will allow to attempt to survive and, if possible, help the others they care about to survive. But as the standard of living in society increases, the time people spend working will diminish while the amount of leisure time they have available to enjoy will increase.

Despite the widespread need to find employment following the economic collapse, some people will have invested intelligently before the collapse and will find themselves in situations where they don't need to work all day. This will be the new wealthy class and we can expect that at first, new entertainment destinations will be catered towards this group.

There have been strict laws against selling sexual acts throughout most of the United States but in the absence of government control, such restrictions will no longer exist. Communities full of landowners who oppose prostitution may restrict such from being offered in their local community, but many landowners will not be opposed to such, and neither will be their employees and customers.

Free markets will revolutionize a sex industry that, until this point, has been largely controlled by black market operators and the few politically connected legal operators who have managed to get the necessary licensing. In the absence of government, anyone with a body can choose to prostitute themselves[6] and anyone with land can choose to let people sell their bodies on it.

The removal of legal restrictions will allow companies with good reputations to enter the sex market and provide safe environments for both sex workers and customers. With the

---

[6] Anyone except people below the age of consent as voted on by contributors to the FSFFW

industry out in the open, violent operators will be quickly discovered and boycotted by both workers and customers, if not sought out and hunted down by those compassionate towards their victims. Given the choice between violent and non-violent environments to work in, most people will choose the non-violent environment, and it is freedom that will provide them with such a choice.

Sex is mysterious in many ways and many people are secretive about their inner desires. There's little way to predict what an entirely free market in sex would result in but it seems to me that the free-for-free hookup culture that exists today would largely be replaced by monetary transactions.

All sexual interactions are economic transactions, even when money does not change hands. Some people are highly in demand with many offers while others can swipe on a dating app for hours with no matches and must settle for whatever crumbs are left over once the highly sought-after have made their selections.

Allowing money to exchange hands can facilitate these transactions and make things more efficient. Instead of "will you sleep with me?" the question becomes "how much must I pay to sleep with you?" The two parties can negotiate with one another and if a deal is made, it will be because each party feels they are receiving more value than they are giving up.

Regardless of whether a person individually supports prostitution, it is a harsh reality that many individuals will be forced to consider it as a means of survival once this economy collapses. For many individuals, the beauty of their physical body is the most precious asset they will possess, and there will be an inclination to capitalize on this value. Prostitution will exist regardless of whether government exists but by removing government restrictions, it can exist in a safer and more controlled setting. Incidents of sexual slavery will diminish greatly and in situations where a person remains enslaved, having legal sex operators throughout the nation will give them additional places they might flee to and be able to support themselves, escaping the grasp of their former captor.

In addition to prostitution, mind-altering drugs and a variety of gambling games will also be accessible in a free society. Humans have become accustomed to the typical games offered by casinos but with freedom, the possibilities will be far greater. Perhaps the winner of the wheel spin gets to have sex with a particularly attractive casino employee. Perhaps men on cocaine will get to bet on voluntary knife fights taking place in a pit. Unbounded by the constraints of government, the imagination can come up with endless possibilities.

As widespread migration occurs, some areas will get built up while other areas will be abandoned. Entertainment destinations that once existed in locations that have now become abandoned will close their doors, just like the many other businesses that once existed in those locations. But in the areas of new development, people will start to demand entertainment and we can expect that new options will appear. Without the constraints of government, there will be few limits as to the experiences that will be for sale and the pleasures that may be enjoyed for the right price.

Charity

Throughout this book, I have at many points claimed that causes should be supported by those who are personally interested in those causes, rather than funded through taxing the entire population. Different people have different priorities and if too few people make an issue a priority to prevent a high risk to society, that issue will eventually make itself known and become a bigger priority.

If insufficient people donate to the FSFFW, it will be unable to respond to all calls for help. If insufficient people donate to the community's fire service, fires will rage out of control. If insufficient people donate to reforestation, the balance of the atmosphere will not be restored. If insufficient people donate to disaster relief, there will be no relief. If people don't donate to public parks, libraries or museums, there will be no free parks, libraries, or museums for the public to visit.

These are harsh potential outcomes, but we can trust that people will donate to the causes they find compelling. Charitable giving in the United States in 2020 was $471 billion according to my quick Google search and this excludes billions more in political donations. People will voluntarily donate to the causes they care about and in the absence of an income tax, combined with economic freedom, people will have much more disposable income to potentially donate.

Not only will people donate out of the compassion in their hearts, but companies will donate to build and maintain a good reputation in the community. If a community is suffering from a lack of fire protection or its roads are in disrepair because no one feels like they can operate them profitably, it will be reasonable to expect that successful businesses in that location contribute some of their profits to address those issues. While there will be no tax authority demanding payment under violent threat, there will be customers prepared to boycott and start shopping with more socially responsible companies. As I have previously mentioned, the more economic prosperity there is, the more people will be enabled to not only address the causes that personally compel them, but also to participate in boycotts.

Once the economic prosperity of society increases to a certain level, it is possible someone will start a charitably funded universal income program to help alleviate the physical burdens people face in our society. There is a concept known as diminishing marginal utility in economics and it tells us that as a person acquires additional units of a particular item, those additional units hold less subjective value to them. This is true not just of goods and services, but also of money itself. A million dollars is worth more to a broke person than to someone who already has a billion dollars.

Because of this, some people with a large amount of wealth may at some point decide that their wealth will be better used by contributing it to a social welfare program that sends out a universal income check to the population. The ideal of socialism where labor becomes unnecessary for most people may someday be achieved through this mechanism, but the contributions to such a program need to be voluntary. Until people reach a level of wealth where they feel like this is the best use of their funds, they should be free to save, invest or otherwise disburse their funds as they see fit.

During an episode in the summer of 2018 that landed me in a mental hospital, I became convinced that Earth was heaven and assumed that heaven's rules were in effect[7]. In heaven, there was so much prosperity that I didn't need to ask to borrow something because there was so much bounty that whoever I wanted to borrow something from wouldn't mind. To ask would be more annoying to them than anything else.

With this mindset, I attempted to enter my neighbor's car, and he reacted by attacking my physically. He choked me out until I was unconscious, and I didn't fight back. I surrendered to the reality of this world as it flooded back into my awareness.

---

[7] Here, I am referring to the heavenly experience I recounted in the Pandora's Box section

73

Regardless of whether I personally consider it moral to take someone else's property without asking, the reality of this world is that people will defend their property claims, with violence if necessary. This book acknowledges that reality and provides a framework through which we can traverse from our current reality to the heavenly state that lies ahead.

At this stage of human evolution, property rights are important, and the FSFFW will ensure they are respected. We live in a world where the material desires of the population are great in relation to the material reality of most people's lives and until this condition has changed, we cannot expect that people will be quick to offer hand-outs to every beggar that shows up at their door. Different people have different priorities as to what are the greatest needs in society and by allowing people to direct their own funds as they see fit, the people most concerned about causes will be the ones directly addressing them, rather than some distant politician squandering the population's money in the ways they personally desire.

Consider the preservation of natural landscapes. Imagine there is an animal migration route and conservationists want to preserve it as a key part of the ecology of the region. By buying up the land over which the migration route passes, the charity owning the land can hold it perpetually, never selling it, regardless of how high the land value gets. Because the charity is funded and controlled by people who care about preserving the natural landscape, it won't be subject to the corrupt incentives that would exist if government controlled the land.

If government was instead assigned to safeguard the environment, there would be no such guarantee. A politician might decide to have the government purchase the land for the purpose of preserving the land but five years later, with a new politician in office, the government's objectives may well change. Perhaps the new politician needs to raise money to cover other government expenditures and a coal company offers the government top dollar to build a railroad across the migration route to transport its coal. The politician may well decide to give up on his predecessor's ecological plan and instead sell the land to the coal company. Had the land instead been owned by a private charity dedicated to environmental conservation, the coal company would have had no chance to acquire it, no matter how high their bid.

Will people fall through the cracks without a government safety net? It will be up to us as compassionate humans to make that decision. Many people in our society have turned a blind eye towards the homeless and other outcasts as they have gone about their daily lives, preferring not to consider the misfortunes of others. At best, they've acknowledged their misfortunes and hoped that government would take care of the problem for them. But with no government available to do so, it will be up to each one of us to become our brother's keeper. My expectation is we will do a far better job of it than government ever has.

Love

Love is unique in that it is not only the most demanded product in our society, but also the one that has been the most mispriced. While other markets, such as the bond market, have had a positive market price with no intrinsic value, love has had a negative market price with intrinsic value higher than any other product. The market for love has been the most mispriced market in our society, and the collapse of this credit bubble will have the most significant impact on love.

I define love as behavior undertaken to benefit others. It is distinct from compassion in that compassion is a desire for others to be benefitted, while love is an action frequently motivated by that desire. But while this is typical, it is also possible to feel compassion without acting out of love, just as it is possible to act in a loving due to a motivator other than compassion. A customer service representative may act in a loving way to serve their customers, but may be motivated by their paycheck, rather than by an inherent feeling of compassion towards said customers. Likewise, a person may feel compassion towards the homeless, but not enough to act in response to that compassion.

Some of the behaviors that are the most beneficial to others, and thus offer the most love, are listening with an intention to understand them and expressing one's own perspective. When I claim love has had a negative market price, it is because individuals have typically suffered for behaving in these ways. Someone who listens to understand has been burdened with understanding the suffering of another. That understanding has typically been combined with an inability to help that individual, because other individuals haven't been interested in listening themselves, and have continued to cause destruction to themselves, despite the desire we have for their pain to be alleviated, once we have heard of their sorrows.

Those who express their own perspective have also been punished, through silencing, ghosting, bullying, and sometimes even physical violence. People have been punished greatly for expressing desires that go against social norms and have even been outcast for expressing pain that no one has cared to listen to.

In the wake of our economic collapse, the demand people have for love will be even higher than it was before the collapse, because the substitutes they have relied upon will become unavailable. There will be a massive amount of pain that, until expressed, will cripple the individuals requiring that expression. There will also be a great demand for the truth about economics, love, God, and the possibilities that lie ahead.

I have created a website where the truths I have come to understand are presented in a blog, and through videos I've recorded that are accessible through the website. I've also linked the channels of other people who I have found to be insightful during the lead-up to this collapse. This material is available without financial cost to those who visit my website, www.humandiscourse.com.

The pain that needs to be expressed needs to be expressed to someone who is trusted by the person expressing it. Many in our society have lost trust and as such, are unlikely to be recipients of such truth. People will take it upon themselves to confess what they will to whom they will but I expect there is a lot more pain on this planet to heal than there are individuals willing and trusted to listen to it. I expect that as a society, we will lack greatly for this variety of love and as such, I believe that Jesus Christ will return to offer us this gift.

Christianity is based upon the story of the Messiah, Jesus Christ, who came here to redeem our species from hell. In exchange for this gift, members of our species decided to execute him, to visit upon the Messiah an unjust punishment of suffering for a being who was pure love. Despite his death sentence, a higher power stepped in to overrule it and three days after his execution, Jesus rose from the dead, presumably healed by the angels who work at the right hand of God. Since that time, the whereabouts of his physical body has been unknown, at least to me. I do not know whether he has been in heaven with the angels or whether he has been undercover here on Earth, but I fully expect he will return to our perspective and offer this species the balance it will require so our marketplace can meet its unfulfilled demand for love.

All humans can offer a degree of love simply by listening to those they intend to love and responding with kindness. Over the past few years, I have engaged in a heavy intellectual discourse with people from all over the political and philosophical spectrum and by listening to them and expressing my honest feedback, I have treated them with love. I am not God, and I am not Jesus, but I am a man capable of a degree of love, as I believe all men to be. When Jesus instructed us, it was to love, and he would not have given us those instructions were we not capable of doing so.

In the new economy, market prices will correct, and love will be rewarded, rather than punished. Those who commit acts of kindness will be rewarded by those who appreciate such acts, without fear that showing such appreciation may result in personal harm. Those who act out of cruelty will be punished not by a centralized government, but by the reactions of their customers, employees, business partners and the general population living in our society. Love will exist not just because people inherently feel compassion but because it will be rewarded. Freedom is the economic structure that will inspire love and will enable us to become the divine beings that our creator intended.

Part III: Ascendance

Angel's Song

I traversed a forest clearing, skipping as you please
When, perchance, I heard some music coming from the trees.

As it played, the melody was that of my own soul.
I sat down and listened as I rested on a bole.

Sweet, seductive words enticed me with their magic song.
Such a pure sound surely could do me no harm or wrong.

Soon, I felt compelled to find out whence this music came.
I got up to look around to try to give it name.

As I rose, the woods became as quiet as can be.
There was no more music playing for the trees or me
.

"Sing for me, you wondrous angel," I implored the sky,
"If I cannot hear you, then I evermore will cry!"

Only silence answered as I looked around in vain,
"Oh, you cannot know how silence brings out all my pain!

I must hear that song for now I know it's part of me!
How can I survive if I must simply stand and be?"

Like a soul possessed, I scurried frantically about.
Sometimes I would cry and sometimes I would want to shout.

Yet, no matter what I did, the singer stayed concealed
And within her silence, slowly truth has been revealed.

If she doesn't want to sing, perhaps she's simply sad.
Perhaps the woods displease her or perhaps they've made her
mad.

After all, the trees are withered, some are even burned.
This is not the land for which humanity has yearned.

Her song, indeed, was meant for me, but it was just a tease.
We must end the violence and we must regrow the trees.

Let us build a paradise where woods are filled with bliss,
Let's make this a land where she finds nothing is amiss.

If we do all this, then maybe she will sing her songs.
For then this will be somewhere that such a sound belongs.

The bounds of collective consciousness

At this point, let us revisit the topic of morality. Many people have discussed the idea of a collective consciousness and many feel like there is such a thing as objective morality. The implication is that through discourse, we might become more like a hive mind regarding morality than individuals with different subjective views of the topic.

A free society will enforce morality through popular opinion and the opinions of those who have wealth will generally be more influential. As time progresses, the moral standards of society are likely to increase as people become more prosperous and are able to afford the luxuries that a more moral life demand. It can thus be said that even if objective morality is true for a given point in time, it will not be true throughout time. The moral standards of society ten years from now are likely to differ from the moral standards of society a hundred years from now.

Yet, even in this current moment, morality still differs. If the median donator to the FSFFW decides the age of consent should be 19, there will be dissenters who think it should be 17 and others who think it should be 21. Not everyone's individual subjective morality will be reflected in the reality that exists in society, even though I have constructed solutions as well as possible to facilitate a peaceful transfer to a new and stable world, and one that will be agreeable to the maximum number of people.

The rules of society should never be mistaken for objective morality but should be viewed more as a subjective morality based on the ideas predominant in society at that time. Those who disagree with those ideas and who support alternative approaches to the existence of the FSFFW should be free to express their concerns and voice their ideas. Those who dislike the practices of other businesses or individuals in society should also be free to speak out, and the accused should be free to defend their behavior or acknowledge their shortcomings without facing violent retribution.

82

Public opinion and the boycott will be powerful tools to direct the moral behavior of humanity in such a way as to continually provide better treatment towards the humans, animals and plants that exist here. I do not expect we will ever arrive at a place of perfect morality because the demands of humans appear endless and if they are, then the kindness one might impart towards them is also endless. So too, I would imagine, are the demands of animals and other more mystical beings that may reemerge[8].

In conclusion, I don't believe objective morality exists or that it will ever exist. Each decision has rewards and potential consequences. While I believe in doing good, there are many situations where we have a decision as to who should be the recipient of that good, and who or what should be sacrificed to obtain it. Sacrifice can result in a greater good, but the motivation should always be that greater good, and never to punish the person being sacrificed. At the end of the day, everyone should be free to make their own decisions as to how their love should be imparted.

Despite a lack of objective morality, it is my hope that my book can provide a mostly agreeable path forward for our society. I have done my best to address the various concerns that people might have regarding a transition to a free society and to facilitate space for everyone to practice their own customs and live in the way that they personally see as morally just. The subtitle of this book is the Bridge to Collective Mind and Spirit and even though I don't believe that objective morality can be discovered, I do believe that we can collectively agree that economic freedom should be the path forward for our society, and engage our spirits towards that objective.

---

[8] These will be discussed in greater detail in the mysticism section

Respect

While the downtrodden have been routinely ignored by our society, the wealthy have typically been held in high esteem. Not only are the wealthy capable of purchasing for us the things we want, but the fact of their wealth may indicate some underlying talent or value that garnished them that wealth.

Unfortunately, the underlying talent all too often in our society has been the ability to control political power. The wealthier classes have used the power of government to favor their business interests at the expense of their competition, and the political class has gotten wealthy alongside them. Too often, an individual's wealth has been representative not of any virtue but of an ability to screw other people over.

In a world where many have struggled for economic survival, it has made sense for people to overlook the shortcomings of the wealthy to remain on their good side and receive the material rewards that doing so may offer. But in doing so, many people have become attached to a social community that is spiritually bankrupt and that will be ill-equipped to handle the times to come. They've placed far too high a value on the merit of these individuals and invested significant time and energy in unhealthy relationships. When the credit bubble collapses, so will the perceived value of many of those individuals who have benefitted the most from that bubble.

In the wake of the collapse, wealth will begin to represent true value rather than an ability to control political power. It will indicate the individual was intelligent enough to understand the economic circumstances we will face and to position themselves for that collapse. As time goes on, wealth will follow those who are able to produce goods or services demanded by society. It will become a better indication of merit than it was in the prior system.

Despite this, it will still not be a perfect indicator. Someone might have gained wealth through inheritance, through luck or through theft. And if respect is granted to people based on their wealth, there will remain a potential they are being socially rewarded for suboptimal behavior.

Respect should be granted to those who we see as engaging in virtuous acts, but there are different levels of respect, and different virtues. Upon meeting someone new, I offer a baseline level of respect which includes consideration of their perspective and basic human decency. So long as they don't take actions that I consider to be cruel, I will maintain that basic level of respect.

If someone takes cruel action, I will withdraw my baseline level of respect until their behavior has been corrected. To me, there is no reason to show respect someone who is cruel and doing so may encourage their cruel behavior to continue.

The opposite of cruel action is heroic action. This is action that goes above and beyond basic human decency and includes an element of self-sacrifice. Examples of heroic action are working hard, taking physical risks, taking emotional risks, or donating money to a charitable cause. When I see or hear about these types of actions, my respect level for an individual increases and now I will not just treat them with basic decency but will also acknowledge their heroism to them and to others that I meet. I will hold them in high esteem.

The ways in which we grant respect are determined by our own morality and as I mentioned in the section on morality, different people have different ideas about morality. It follows that they also have different views about what is respectable behavior.

To me, no other individual's respect means as much to me as my self-respect. No one else knows me as well as I know myself, and no one else understands the reasons for the behaviors I've undertaken better than I know them myself. While I listen to the feedback others have to offer and appreciate when they can show me my blind spots, I don't accept their overall judgement of me as reality. It's frequently just conjecture based on their limited vantage point. Either they can illuminate something I don't see about myself, and I can determine if my

85

behavior needs to be corrected, or they can't. If they can't, then I don't need to lose sleep over whatever judgements they are arriving at based on their fear, ignorance, and refusal to look at things objectively.

By adjusting how we grant respect away from material wealth and towards quality of character, we can inspire good behavior in those around us. Even if people do not inherently feel the compassion that may inspire good behavior, they will act in ways that are kind because they will be socially rewarded for doing so. And just as boycotts of a company's products may inspire a company towards better behavior, boycotts of affection and respect towards cruel individuals may inspire them to the same.

Families

Our children are the future, and my children are the reason I have remained on this planet for as long as I have. Over the past few years, I have traversed a journey of extraordinary emotional pain and on many days, I have wished not to awaken. Despite this, I have carried on, placing one foot in front of the other, and I have done it for them.

We have relied upon a government system of adoption and foster homes that has been dubious at best. Many children have failed to be placed into caring homes while many capable parents have been unable to jump through the necessary government hoops to adopt.

In the absence of government, children will be free to leave bad caretakers to go live with better ones. The FSFFW will not be responding to kidnapping calls unless those being kidnapped are being confined with or sexually abused by their new custodians. If they are free to come and go as they wish and have voluntarily left their parents to live with custodians they judge to be better, the FSFFW will not be involved.

It may seem harsh that bad parenting will result in children abandoning their parents, but children should be free to escape abusive homes. Parents who are treating their children poorly are either unwilling or unable to tend to their children's needs. Freeing their children to leave to find a better home will unburden those who do not wish to be parents, or are incapable of being good ones.

It will fall upon those of us in society who do care about children to open our homes or donate to orphanages that can adopt unwanted children. Some children may decide they want to work for an employer and live without any adult supervision, and this should also be permitted. As long as they are following the general rules of society that apply to everyone, as enforced by the FSFFW, they should not create any problems.

We have been operating in a complex legal web relating to child custody, child support and spousal maintenance. None of this is necessary. People should contribute financially to those children they care about and those in society who care about children should step up for those children who are uncared for. Parental assignments should not be determined just by blood but by love. Those who care for children should be those who are paying for them and raising them.

This will likely have the effect of putting many women in a position where they are responsible for raising their children without relying on financial support from the children's father. Knowing this risk exists should cause women to use an increased amount of discretion when deciding who to have sex with and what birth control mechanisms to use. With free market medicine, birth control pills will be available over the counter for cheap prices, as will condoms and other preventative birth control measures. Abortion will be permitted for fetuses below the age of life as determined by the vote of contributors to the FSFFW.

This should inspire those who care about women's health to contribute to charitable organizations that can provide sexual education and birth control distribution. Like other charitable causes, economic freedom will empower people to earn the maximum income with which they can contribute to those causes that they find the most compelling.

I was unhappily married for eight years to my children's mother and am now a single parent. After a tumultuous journey of marriage where things seemed to get consistently worse, I fell for another woman and experienced an emotional affair that showed me how much this universe had to offer, and that I was lacking. I realized I did not marry my wife out of love but out of an obligation to check the boxes society encouraged me to check. When I discovered real love, it shattered my acceptance of my current reality and inspired the tremendous emotional, intellectual, and spiritual journey that I have been on for the past few years.

While the woman I fell for departed my life, a flame within me was lit and I took a deep delve into the nature of women to try to determine what I needed to do to obtain the joy that had

88

eluded me. One conclusion I've arrived at is that while she may have offered me bliss, others also have gifts to offer. I would like to experience those gifts and can no longer envision a future with a single woman where I am monogamous.

People have diverse viewpoints on the topic of monogamy versus polyamory. Non-religious people seem to have little moral imperative to be monogamous and some religions allow for specific forms of polygamy. In the Quran, it is said that a man may marry "two or three or four women", so long as he can treat them with equal fairness. Certain sects of Mormonism have a similar approach.

Other religions strictly forbid relationships outside of one man and one woman. I mentioned my belief in Jesus earlier in this book, but this belief has been insufficient to convince me that monogamy is the only ethical practice in this world. Jesus himself indicated that the rules in heaven may be different, and as someone who expects we will transform this planet into a heavenly state, I also expect our rules regarding relationships may change.

Despite all this, I currently have zero romantic partners, and have had none since the time of my divorce. The right connection or connections have not yet appeared in my life, and I do not know what, if anything, may lie in store for me romantically. My priority remains creating a good life for my two children who I love dearly and would like to see prosper in this world.

A free society is likely to result in many different types of family structures and living arrangements. Out of economic necessity, we will likely see multiple traditional families cohabitating under one roof in the days to come, and we will likely also see polyamorous groups form where children are raised by the community. In a free society, like-minded people can do things the way they want on the land they own and different tribes can do things different ways on their own land. So long as no one is enslaving anyone, having sexual relations with a child below the age of consent, or violating the property rights of others, people will be free to do as they see fit.

Generalizations

Our minds constantly seek patterns to help them make sense of the universe around us. We look for patterns and once we observe them, we begin to consider them laws of the universe, at least until contrary evidence presents itself.

There are many observations we can make about the individuals around us including their skin color, gender, age, and accent. From talking with them, we can gain additional information regarding their nationality, political party, personal preferences, vaccination status, and other criteria.

We can choose to take such information and use it to make assumptions regarding that individual's intelligence, ability to have empathy or show compassion, behavior, beliefs, preferences, motives, talent, or their general value as a human being. Such a judgement might be based on a history of interactions with individuals sharing that common characteristic, or it might be based on people we've trusted proclaiming the generalization in question to be correct. Regardless of how we came to believe the generalization, judging other people in this way is very problematic.

The first and most obvious problem is that not all instances of people in the given group will share the assigned characteristic. If we make an errant assumption, it may prevent us from gaining an appreciation of the true value of the individual by causing us to dismiss their ideas or behavior as unworthy of full consideration. If I assume that a different class of people than myself is stupid, then why should I be interested in their ideas? If I assume that a different class of people than me lacks empathy, then why should I express my honest feelings? If I assume that a different class of people than me lacks compassion, then why should I make towards them an emotional appeal? If I assume that a different class of people than me lacks a particular interest, motive, or talent, I may miss an economic opportunity that would have been a win-win situation. If I assume that a different class of people knows something or doesn't know something, I may be leaving them without critical information or wasting time explaining something they already understand.

Additionally, when we make assumptions about other individuals, especially negative assumptions, we will offend them when we are incorrect (and frequently even when we are correct). By acting in an offensive manner, we will lose our credibility in their eyes, and, likely, they will begin to make negative assumptions about us, or various groups of which we are a part. Whatever points we wanted to make will be lost, and, unless the purpose of our dialogue was to offend, our purpose will be unfulfilled.

People generalize a lot and my intention in writing this is not to condemn those people so much as to present a rational take as to why their approach is flawed. Generalizations fuel hatred, and hatred fuels violence. As someone who wants to live in a peaceful world, it is incumbent upon me to draw attention to this flawed approach to judgement.

It is better to evaluate someone as an individual, rather than as a part of a whole. But even in evaluating someone as an individual, it is important not to generalize regarding that specific individual. Just because a person has presented one errant conclusion does not mean that every conclusion they will present is errant. Just because a person engaged in cruel behavior in one instance does not mean every behavior that person has ever taken has been cruel. Just because a person once failed to have empathy does not mean they always will. It is not just each individual, but each action of each individual, that should be evaluated independently.

Once this is done, we soon discover that it is difficult, if not impossible, to find a perfect hero or a perfect villain. Thomas Jefferson stood against a tyrannical government and yet he was a slave-owner. Martin Luther King, Jr. advanced the cause of nonviolent social change yet failed to understand how free-market capitalism could take us to the promised land. People are mixed bags, and no one I've become aware of is flawless.

92

Despite this, there are heroes amongst us. I defined heroism in the respect section of this book as action that goes above and beyond human decency, and which involved a sacrifice of oneself. Jesus suffering on the cross was a great example of heroism, as have been the sacrifices of all those who have died for that which they have believed in. A behavior does not have to be objectively moral to be heroic, for objective morality has not been discovered. It only must involve self-sacrifice for the sake of others and I can consider a person's actions to be heroic while also considering it to be destructive.

I consider both Thomas Jefferson and Martin Luther King Jr. heroes for the personal hardships and risks they undertook for that which they believed in. I consider soldiers who risk their lives for the sake of a belief doing so will protect their country to be heroes. I consider firefighters who enter burning buildings to rescue others to be heroes. I consider police officers who risk their lives for the sake of keeping their communities safe to be heroes. I consider single parents who bust their asses every day to put food on the table for their children to be heroes.

Libertarians who came before me and taught the lessons of freedom to the world are heroes to me, for they have had to suffer the pain of having their viewpoints suppressed and silenced from mainstream conversation while the world burns and the ideas they have offered have fallen upon deaf ears. Ron Paul is a hero to me. Ludwig Von Mises is a hero to me. Murray Rothbard is a hero to me. Ayn Rand is a hero to me. Peter Schiff is a hero to me. The other commentators I link on my website at www.humandiscourse.com are heroes to me.

All the great human thinkers are heroes to me, for they have challenged the ideas of their day at the cost of great personal effort and suffering. They have been outcast, they have been silenced, they have been ridiculed, they have been de-funded, they have been bullied, and they have been exiled. At times, they have been executed for the fear of the ruling authority has been so great that such horror has been their only chance to maintain power.

Still, their ideas have remained, and new thinkers have picked up where they left off. I consider myself to be a hero for writing this book, for delving into the ideas of some of humanity's best thinkers and constructing a solution through which our species can walk to freedom. Yet, I also am not perfect.

Over the course of my lifetime, I have bullied others, I have assaulted them, I have stolen their property, I have vandalized their property and I have endangered their lives. I have said things that have caused people great emotional distress and I have killed animals for sport. Beyond my known offenses, I have acted out of ignorance and harmed people in ways I have later discovered, but also in ways that I surely remain ignorant of.

I have not achieved perfection and am only human, a servant of God, and a man who believes his book can heal this world from the sickness it has been suffering from. I am a hero in my own eyes because I know the suffering I have walked through to get to this point, and the sacrifices I have made so my children may see a better tomorrow. I also recognize that I'm not alone amongst human heroes and believe that given the right opportunity and the love that exists deep within all human hearts, anyone is capable of heroism.

Foreign Nations

In a sense, foreign individuals and governments will have gotten the short end of the stick with the declaration that all debts payable in U.S. dollars are now worthless, for they have held much of that debt. The unfortunate reality is they invested in something that was highly overvalued, the credit of Americans. Part of the risk a creditor undertakes when selling a bond is a devaluation of the currency in which that bond is payable. Creditors of these debt instruments made a bet on the U.S. dollar, and they lost.

While the default of our nation's debt may seem regretful to such individuals, it at least signifies an end of a system from which they have greatly suffered. People around the world have worked hard to produce the products Americans and others in debtor nations have consumed and in return, they've been given IOUs payable in a currency that has or will become worthless. Their losses cannot be recovered, but their escape from a tyrannical world order is imminent and hopefully they will make better investment decisions as we move into the future.

While the debt they were holding may have been canceled, the productive facilities of nations will remain. If their governments are intelligent, they will undergo a similar plan of liquidation as the United States government and allow free markets to determine how their remaining capital should be allocated. Losing one's biggest customer hurts a business tremendously and many foreign businesses may need to substantially restructure or liquidate to adjust to changing global demands. Removing government red tape will allow this process to happen efficiently and ease the economic suffering of their populations.

We have lived in a world of numerous physical conflicts between nations and the United States government has stationed troops throughout the world, involving itself in a great many conflicts overseas. Upon the collapse of the credit bubble, the U.S. government will no longer be able to fund these military

95

campaigns and there will need to be a withdrawal of troops from around the world.

As we saw from the debacle of the Afghanistan withdrawal, it is important to consider the ramifications of such an event, especially regarding those individuals who have sided with U.S. troops and who may suffer from their withdrawal.

To facilitate withdrawals that are peaceful and orderly to the greatest extent, all interested parties should engage in discourse to determine agreements as to the withdrawal. Without doing such, it will be impossible to understand the desires of foreign parties and without understanding those desires, it will be impossible to design solutions whereby both their interests and our own are considered.

For some time on my YouTube channel, I have discussed the state of Israel and the precarious position it is likely to find itself in once U.S. military and economic support must, by economic necessity, be withdrawn. Many parties in this world have found the Israeli treatment of the Palestinian people to be abhorrent and once the U.S. withdraws from the region, there is a strong likelihood that efforts will be made by others in the Muslim world to liberate Palestine from what they see as Israeli invaders of their land.

It is futile to get caught up in whether Israel or Palestine's claim to the territory is morally higher, the only factor that is relevant for practical consideration is who will have the power to claim that territory. At the current time, Israel has the power, largely due to the economic and military support of the western world. But, once that support collapses, the balance of power is likely to shift.

While Israel has a significant military presence of its own and a significant amount of farmland that may be used to produce and sustain an economy, it is a small nation and will likely be up against a larger force that will be bankrolled by Iranian oil. Their ability to keep their borders secure and to protect their productive agricultural facilities will be in great doubt when faced with such an enemy.

96

Even if Israel is successful in holding off the initial assault, they can expect continued aggression. The opposing force will have a good chance of being able to surround the country, cutting off trade and crippling whatever economy might remain once the U.S. credit bubble has collapsed. Over time, it seems impossible that they will hold their position and not eventually succumb to the invading force.

Because the invaders will be fueled by a hatred based on the injustices perceived by many in the region regarding the Palestinians and other groups in the middle east who have been targeted by the western world, it is likely that if they successfully invade Israel that they will show little to no mercy to the population. The infamous holocaust of World War II may pale in comparison to what will be done to any residents that are trapped there.

At the current time, Israel maintains a bargaining chip, because they maintain economic and political power over the territory. At the current time, they can offer freedom to their citizens, and equal freedom to the citizens of Palestine. They can acknowledge where they have been cruel, they can set to right the harm they have done, and they can lay themselves before those they have oppressed with a hope that they will be shown mercy in return for this act of kindness.

The window to do so is closing and there will likely come a point where it is too late for such an offer. No one is interested in hearing an apology that is uttered simply to attempt to avoid punishment. Victims desire a meaningful gesture to accompany the apology, and pre-emptively offering freedom to the Palestinians would be a real heartfelt gesture that would improve the lives of innocent people who are suffering in this world.

It seems highly unlikely the government of Israel will read this and decide to do as I propose, because I do not expect them to be fully aware of the economic events to come, nor cognizant of the hopelessness they will be faced with once those events come to pass. Yet, I write these words anyway, both for the miniscule chance they will make a difference in this circumstance and for the greater purpose of showing the world that this is the correct way to behave. Perhaps I cannot convince this oppressor to cease their abuse but perhaps upon witnessing what ultimately happens to the state of Israel, future potential oppressors will read these words and pay heed to their wisdom.

I do not know to what extent the Israeli regime would be forgiven if they were to pre-emptively facilitate such a transition, nor do I know what types of violence they might face were they to allow Hamas free roam on their streets. All I can point attention to is how hopeless their situation will be when the dollar collapses.

In the "collapse" section of this book, I discussed my own experience with alcoholism and how I needed to be faced with hopelessness to make a change. I was fortunate in that my drinking got bad enough to show me my hopelessness before it killed me. Many alcoholics are not so fortunate, and it is my expectation that many in this world will not reach the point of hopelessness until it is too late to save them.

While hopelessness may inspire spiritual action, it is not necessary to become hopeless to take such action. I was once taught a spiritual technique that I rarely hear spoken about, even in the most advanced spiritual circles I find myself within. That technique is to ask God for willingness.

There are times when a hatred is so great that we cannot find it within ourselves to ask God to remove that hatred from us, and where an intermediate step is necessary. The step is to pray for the willingness to have him remove from us that part of us with which we are greatly identified, but which we know in the grand scheme of things to be harmful to our spiritual condition.

I hold no animosity towards Jewish people. Like all other people, I consider them as individuals, rather than a part of a whole. I don't want to see those individuals slaughtered, but I fear this is a result we are headed towards with reckless abandonment. Hopefully, individuals reading these words can either affect a change in the policies of the Israeli government or

98

convince as many Israelis as possible to flee the country before this seemingly inevitable genocide occurs.

Beyond Israel, we have a world full of governments that exert various levels of control over their populations. By creating a free society in America, we will not only be providing a potential refuge for those suffering around the world under the oppression of tyrannical governments, but we will show the world an example of what a free society and economy can look like. Over time, our society will become more and more prosperous and peaceful, and I expect individuals around the world will see this and start to demand their own freedoms.

The FSFFW will act to prevent trespassing, but this does not mean they will provide troops to prevent people from crossing the borders into the region formerly known as the United States[9]. They will be on call to respond if individual landowners are experiencing trespassers but if an individual wants to welcome foreigners onto their land, the FSFFW will not seek to prevent this.

Regarding the many areas of former U.S. border owned by governments, it will not be up to the FSFFW, but up to the liquidation estate of that government to determine which people should be allowed on that land. If they feel it is in the best interest of the population not to allow the public, or individuals who were not legal U.S. residents, onto that land, they can engage the services of the FSFFW to enforce that decision.

If the purpose of restricting trespassers to that land is to prevent damage to that land from littering or vandalism, it seems that the liquidation estate will be rational if it decides to restrict access to that land, allowing them to maintain the value of that land and maximizing the ultimate amount of proceeds that will be received by the population. But if the purpose is because foreigners are not trusted to be peaceful, the effort is likely to be futile.

---

[9] Or the greater free world if it has expanded beyond just the region formerly known as the United States.

Once we allow each landowner to determine who should be allowed on their land, it will become very easy for any landowner sympathetic to foreign terrorist organizations to welcome terrorists onto their land and to bypass any restrictions the government's liquidation estate has regarding its own land. The safety of society will be ensured not by a strong border, but by a strong and efficient FSFFW that will efficiently and effectively stamp out threats that appear.

This will be supplemented by a free-market justice system. Just because the FSFFW is not engaged to seek justice for crimes that have already been committed does not mean the population will not take matters into its own hands. If a group decides to launch an attack, successfully bypasses whatever private security measures are in place, and completes the act and escapes before the FSFFW can respond, that means a retaliatory attack against them from other interests in society also has a good chance of being successful.

Those who enter our society with violent intent will discover that free market justice is far more efficient, effective, and just than the government monopoly it will replace. Those inclined towards violence may be successful in their initial attacks but will almost certainly meet a grizzly end eventually. Recall that justice insurance will likely to be offered as a product by those with a reputation for dispatching that justice efficiently and effectively.

Violence occurs for reasons that are understandable and, for the most part, avoidable. Many have turned to violence out of economic necessity but with a free market, such people will have nonviolent opportunities to survive and prosper. Many have turned to violence to control political power but in the absence of such power, there will be no further reason for this violence.

Much violence has also been attributed to religious extremism, the idea that there are individuals who will kill because they believe that is God's will. Such individuals may be willing to face any Earthly consequences of their actions because they believe they will be rewarded in the afterlife. While there may be some individuals inclined towards religious extremism, there are reasons to believe this threat will not be as severe as some may expect.

From the perspective of young men living in the Middle East, the United States has for their entire lives been a military presence in their region, contributing to the widespread conflicts and suffering that has occurred there. It has been very easy for extremist organizations to recruit members while painting the United States as a great evil that needs to be abolished.

With the Federal government stepping aside, giving up its power, and withdrawing troops from around the world, the enemy that has been causing this suffering will have been eliminated. It has not been the American people that have been the enemy for the American people are a diverse group of individuals with many religions and political beliefs, including many Muslims. It has been the corrupt political establishment that has been the problem and without their aggression in the picture, we can begin to hope for a day where we can meet those who have stood against us as human brethren.

I cannot compel forgiveness from any side of the conflicts that have taken place, as all sides have suffered great losses and forgiveness is a personal journey. However, I can say that all sides would benefit from a peaceful society and by creating such a society in America, it will be harder to justify painting us as the enemy. Not only this, but with free markets we will soon become an economic powerhouse and bullying us will be ill advised. Foreign nations and groups will benefit greatly from trading with us once we are exporting real products instead of bonds payable in a soon-to-be worthless currency. Disrupting those relationships for the sake of imparting violence will be a lose-lose situation for everyone involved.

Once our economy is booming, people will begin to contribute to the causes they care about. At first, there will be tremendous need for charity in many areas as many individuals find themselves in desperate situations and the ecology of our planet faces grave threats. But as time continues and productivity continues, those causes will be addressed, freeing the excess wealth of society up to address additional causes.

Many in our society feel empathy towards those living under totalitarian regimes and once people have sufficient purchasing power available to them, they will likely begin to fund missions to rescue the oppressed and dispatch of their oppressors, no matter where in the world the activity is happening. The FSFFW will only be responsible for securing the free world and so whatever activity is taking place in foreign nations will not be their concern. Violence tends to beget violence and foreign governments continuing to use violence to control their populations can expect that eventually, privately funded retaliation will be likely to occur.

Technology

A termination of intellectual property laws will do a great amount to inspire the development and use of technology. Every invention that humankind has come up with will be available for anyone who wants to use or further develop that technology to administer a productive process. It will not only increase the productivity of society, but it will force manufacturers to compete on reputation rather than through using political or legal means to restrict their competition.

While intellectual property advocates have reasonably pointed out that a financial incentive can inspire the efforts necessary to develop new technology, I mentioned when discussing drug patents in the healthcare section that such a financial incentive does not have to be offered through restricting economic competition. Like other societal objectives previously sought through government action, the objective of inspiring the efforts to develop new technology can be achieved through private charity.

By offering prizes or wages for the developers of technology, a charitable organization can achieve the objective of inspiring research and development without also harming the overall economy and creating corrupt incentives. Other charities can offer prizes to inspire works of music, literature and other artistic endeavors that will then enter the public domain.

Technology can be used to do good or to harm others but by terminating government regulations and allowing markets to work efficiently, consumers will reward producers that improve their lives while punishing those that harm people. If only three companies receive government patents to produce vaccines and all three are shown to be corrupt companies that produce dangerous products, people may still take those vaccines and thus endanger themselves if they are panicking about a virus. Without government restrictions, anyone can produce a vaccine or alternative treatment and whoever has the best safety results will win market share.

In the absence of government restrictions, I expect people will be shocked at how accessible technology becomes and how fast it develops. Products that people are accustomed to being expensive luxuries will plumet in price and become affordable to those with more modest means. Advancements in technology will continuously revolutionize the way we conduct our businesses and lives.

Space travel may stall for some time as we address the more immediate problems that exist here on Earth and build for ourselves a strong foundation in this universe. But human curiosity is endless and with the eventual prosperity that will come, so will return the desire to voyage into space.

As we deplete the finite resources of our planet, we will likely investigate space to supplement our supply of them. Missions for the purpose of harvesting resources will launch based on supply and demand. At the point that it becomes marginally more profitable to harvest resources from nearby asteroids than to purchase them on Earth, we will start to see a great expansion in our space exploration that is driven by profit rather than mere curiosity.

Yet, asteroids are only the first step in our exploration of the cosmos. Someday, humans will likely walk on Mars and charitably or private-funded missions should be expected to continue the exploration of our solar system. Yet, even our own solar system is unlikely to contain our species in perpetuity once we have freedom.

At the current time, physicists believe it to be impossible for anything to exceed the speed of light[10] but they also will concede that Einstein's theory of general relativity is yet to be reconciled with our understanding of quantum mechanics. While both theories seem to consistently hold true in experimental data, they cannot both be true, for they contradict one another. Our

---

[10] With the possible exception of communication during quantum entanglement

understanding of the physical laws of our universe remains incomplete.

Those who have had profound mystical experiences through psychedelic drugs or deep states of meditation have come to understand that the physical world we perceive is but the surface level of a far greater reality that exists. On several occasions in my life, I have smoked extracts of the plant salvia divinorum that grows in an isolated mountain region in Mexico. Upon smoking this plant, I have felt convinced that I am experiencing something akin to a dream, and that a greater reality exists beyond my perception.

I have also become convinced that love is not just a function of brain chemicals but is fundamentally intertwined with the laws that govern this universe. At times, I have felt as though I've been on the verge of understanding these laws and being able to express them in mathematical form. Their structure has just slightly eluded me, and my understanding has been lost as I have returned from the effects of the plant. Despite this, I am convinced that such laws exist and I expect that once discovered, they will refute not only the laws of thermodynamics as we currently understand them, but the barrier of the speed of light. And I expect that the angels, mentioned in a later section, are aware of these laws.

If humankind gains an understanding of these laws, the barriers that keep us confined to our own solar system are likely to be removed as we discover an entire galaxy to potentially be explored.

Mysticism

Even without developing additional technology, we already have the tools to create a paradise here, if our tools can be put to good use. We can grow as many trees as are necessary to restore ecological balance to our environment and some individuals may even choose to live in said trees. Throughout my travels, I have met several individuals inclined towards forest life but restricted by government from the opportunities that would enable it. With freedom, those with sufficient capital could own their own forests and introduce whatever kind of wildlife they want to those forests, including feral human beings.

I once met a woman who expressed a desire to live as a wood nymph, spending her time naked in a pond with other nymphs. By harnessing the power of human technology, such a living environment could be created and sustained. The landowner could pay for security and perhaps even charge admission to eager young adults seeking to explore the forest in search of the legendary nymphs.

Trees themselves have a mystical quality and I have personally engaged in several conversations with them. Through the authoring of this book, they have only responded with silence, but silence is a powerful form of communication that can contain wisdom. Tales from antiquity tell of times when the trees could talk, including the oaks of the Dodona that were said in Greek mythology to contain the gift of prophecy. Alexander the Great was said to have visited a talking a tree, and when the prophet Muhammad spoke, he was said to have stood by a date palm tree that would weep at his words. Perhaps trees stopped talking when humans stopped listening but as we restore the forests of this world, we cannot know what mystical wonders we may behold.

Many legends tell tales of other mystical creatures that once inhabited this planet, a group known as elementals. From the mermaids of the ocean to the fairies of the forest, there seems to be a common romantic desire for humans to encounter that which is extraordinary. While such tales may seem far-fetched to those of us who have lived metropolitan lives, nature has maintained an amount of mystery despite humankind's attempts to gain complete dominion over it.

On this planet, we still have an ocean that is largely unexplored. We have an entire continent covered by an ice sheet millions of square miles in area and thousands of feet thick. We have species deep within the Amazon rainforest that have been undiscovered. We have areas of vast wilderness rarely visited by humans, and where great secrets may be hidden. Our world continues to contain extraordinary mysteries, despite our exploration and occasional arrogance to think we are aware of all that is here.

Many humans have claimed to possess mystical powers such as clairvoyance and clairaudience. Yogis such as those described in Paramahansa Yogananda's famous book, "Autobiography of a Yogi" have been described as having mystical abilities such as the ability to teleport or levitate. In my own life, I have experienced a particular ability to detect the presence of other individuals in the room without seeing them, and to react without conscious thought to the emotional states of those around me.

Such abilities can inspire fear in those unfamiliar with them and for a large portion of recorded history, the western world has been run by churches that have tended to explain away any such phenomenon as satanic possession. Practitioners have been accused of heresy, hunted down, and burned at the stake. Even in the modern world, someone claiming mystical powers is more likely to be ridiculed and confined within a mental institution than accepted, acknowledged, and listened to. For these reasons, it is likely that anyone in our world capable of demonstrating such powers has been reluctant to do so. Similarly, any species that once cohabitated our planet and displayed such abilities has likely been hunted down by our predecessors and either killed or driven into hiding.

I believe God cares about us, for I cannot conceive of a being creating love without himself being a kind being. Through numerous circumstances in my own life that have seemed far more than coincidental, I have come to believe there is a divine plan orchestrating the events of our world. While humans have been granted the autonomy to act as they will within the confines of the circumstances they exist in and have unfortunately caused great amounts of suffering with this freedom, I believe God and his angels have intervened many times throughout history, and throughout my personal life, to bring us all to the place where we currently stand. I believe he is running this show and I believe that as we transition our society from one of cruelty to one of kindness, we may gradually start to regain the trust of those mystics and mystical creatures that have gone into hiding.

Beautiful women also seem to contain within them a mystical power that is recognized by many and yet accepted without a great amount of additional scrutiny. I seem to let them get away with things and I sometimes feel hesitant to question their motives for how could something so beautiful have cruel intentions?

In the western world, this mysticism has historically been attributed to the glory of God and to an incredible gift he has given us, one that may be displayed for the world to see but only enjoyed by her husband within a marriage.

In much of the Islamic world, the beauty of women has been hidden from public view as women have been required to cover themselves fully except within their home. Yet, even within Islam, the power of female beauty is still acknowledged. It is my understanding that certain sects of Islam believe good men will be rewarded with beautiful women in heaven. It is also my understanding that the Quran permits a man to enjoy not only the physical company of his wife or wives, but also of his concubines.

Romantic desire is a powerful motive, and I do not believe I would have been able to withstand the pain of this desire unfulfilled without the help of God. While my desire has not diminished, I believe it is God's presence in my life that has caused me to prioritize kindness over physical intimacy, and to act with kindness towards all, regardless of whether I am romantically attracted to them.

For all I have studied women in hopes of receiving the mystical promise they offer, I remain in a state of ignorance regarding many of their motives. Their psyche remains an impenetrable boundary, one that may perhaps reveal more of itself in time, but one that I expect will never fully be revealed.

I expect it is the same way with other mystical beings and discoveries. God has given us a dynamic and infinite universe to play with, and I don't expect there will be a singularity reached where all is known. Regardless of how much we learn, we will remain ignorant of the infinite amount of information that it outside our current perspective. Through this gift, life can remain interesting and exciting, even once we live in a world that has transcended violence.

Reptilians

If we look back over the history of humankind, we will see our species has gradually gained dominion over our planet, driving many other large species into extinction, and rising to the top of the food chain. It has not been through sheer physical strength that we have done so, but through a combination of our opposable thumbs, ability to walk upright, large brains, and ability to use language. Species have competed on this planet for millions of years with varying traits, but this combination seems to result in an ultimately unstable state where the dominant species becomes so dominant that it finds itself struggling to feed itself and provide itself with a good standard of living. Without a grounded understanding of economics and a willingness of people to donate to an organization such as the FSFFW to enforce a free society, such a resourceful species seems ultimately doomed.

One of the great mysteries of our world is how the dinosaurs disappeared. While some attribute their extinction to an asteroid strike or volcanic activity that resulted in large changes to the climate, is it possible that this climate change was caused not by either of these but by the actions of an intelligent species that lived on this planet?

If a species of intelligent reptiles lived at the time of the dinosaurs, is it possible that they may physically have evolved to develop similar characteristics as humans such as the ability to walk upright, use language, and grasp things with their hands? And is it possible that they also became the dominant species on the planet, wiping out the large dinosaurs that roamed the land to consume their meat as food?

Perhaps they arrived at a point where there were no dinosaurs left to eat, and saw the writing on the wall. Perhaps their scientists determined that the only way for them to survive would be to freeze themselves within ice for millions of years to allow small species to develop into the large mammals that roamed the planet in the early days of humanity. Or, perhaps most of the reptilians' numbers died off and only a small group

110

remained through the millennia, hunting whatever they could to survive, and escaping the notice of the humans that ultimately evolved on this planet.

Is it possible that such a group of reptilians may have developed the ability to shape shift or disguise themselves in such a way as to appear human? David Icke is a man who has been seeking deep truths about our society for decades and while I am not greatly familiar with his work, it is my understanding that he has presented a significant amount of evidence with relation to the reptilian theory. At the least, it seems like something that should be explored further.

During my supposed mental health episode in 2018, I came to believe for a short time in shape shifting. While the idea of shape-shifting humanoid reptilians may seem like one from a horror movie script, the idea has reappeared frequently in the imagination of many story tellers over time, and they're typically seen as an evil species. Might some of the stories that created these legends have been based on reality?

In the garden of Eden, it was said to be a serpent that tempted Adam and Eve with the forbidden fruit. Typical snakes don't talk, so this seems to indicate some kind of intelligent species of reptile. Furthermore, it seems that at least this member of that species intended to cause much suffering for ours.

Why would the reptilians want to harm us? Perhaps they concluded that turning our planet into a farm of intelligent humans could provide them with food and whatever other pleasures they desire. Perhaps some of these pleasures would seem horrific to us and they have come to see us as the enemy because we would deny them such delights.

With the awakening of humanity, freedom is inevitable. Our structures of government will come undone with the collapse of government's ability to fund its expenditures and those who would seek to dominate others through those structures will fail in that undertaking, regardless of whether they are human or reptilian. All I can suggest for any reptilians alive on this planet is to confess your wrongdoings, your desires, and your nature to us and to God. Offer yourselves into God's service and place yourself at his mercy. I have also been a sinful creature in my life and his mercy seems to have been great enough for me.

Angels

One of the observations of chaos theory is that of self-similarity. It seems that everything that exists in the universe exists in multiple similar forms but that each exact form is slightly different. This is true of rocks, trees, rivers, planets, stars, galaxies, moons, clouds, humans, dogs, snowflakes, and skin cells. It appears to be true of everything that exists in the natural universe with one glaring exception which is life-bearing planets. As far as we have discovered, our planet is unique in the universe regarding life's existence on it.

While we have only observed a miniscule fraction of the planets in the universe, it seems surprising that no life has been discovered. For a century, our species has been emitting radar transmissions from our planet that have been traveling out at the speed of light since then, giving us a detectable signature in the universe with a circumference of approximately 200 light-years. Thousands of stars exist within that sphere and if intelligent life exists within that sphere, it has likely detected our presence by now.

A strong radar signal could potentially travel for hundreds of additional light years and remain detectable. And, if any species within a few hundred light-years were emitting such signals themselves, it seems we would have detected them by now. It seems that either the self-similarity principle of chaos theory has an exception, or that intelligent life is so rare that it doesn't exist close enough to be detectable.

Another possibility is that intelligent alien life does exist within that sphere, but that it has made the conscious decision not to reveal its presence to us. Such a decision seems rational if this alien life is intelligent enough to be aware of how we have treated one another on this planet. Ask the Native Americans whether they think it would be a good idea for a peaceful alien species to notify us of their presence.

Humans can accomplish anything they set their mind to, and the detection of an alien species may drive humanity in a single-minded objective to eliminate that threat. Consider the widespread paranoia and irrational behavior that has resulted from the supposed coronavirus threat. If an invisible virus that has killed less than 1 percent of those it has infected can create a global panic that has lasted for as long as this one has, what kind of panic might the detection of an alien species create?

In almost every religious tradition, there is some mention of angels or angelic-type beings. While the stories differ from one culture and part of the world to another, descriptions of beings that descend from the heavens, fly with their wings, and emit light are commonalities that resurface in many traditions. Such beings are said to have descended from heavens, performed miraculous feats, and then departed, leaving us with only their legends.

Earlier in this book, I spoke of love as an economic market. I described it as the product that is most in demand in our society. It is the satisfaction of longing, the gateway to heaven, and the tear in one's eye. Tears are a physical manifestation of love and whenever a person cries, they should be aware that they cry for love. We shed tears because we are separated from the warmth that we once knew, the place from which we came, and the place to which we are destined to return.

Humans have sacrificed for the sake of love for as long as they have walked on this planet. Everyone who works to provide for their family sacrifices for the sake of love. Everyone who has been punished for standing against tyranny has sacrificed for the sake of love. Everyone who has died for a political cause they've believed in has died for the sake of love.

Yet, there are sacrifices greater than death, and the fact of suicides that have occurred to escape from emotional pain prove it. Love may demand exile from one's home and friends. It may demand humiliation, imprisonment, or physical and emotional torture. It may require years of hardship, ostracization by one's community, loss of one's prestige, money, family, friends, and occupation. It may require a person to abstain from food as Gandhi did or it may require one to suffer on a cross as Jesus did. For Jesus, death was not the sacrifice but the reward, for he would rise to join the angels. The sacrifice was the physical torture he experienced prior to that point.

Romantic love is a particular type of love. It is the type of love that songwriters and poets speak of. While all love is founded in innocence, romantic love involves physical desire coupled with that innocence. It is perhaps the highest form of love, for it the form of love that seems to require the greatest sacrifice to manifest.

Romantic love demands sacrifice in the greatest of emotional ways, and a great many suicides have resulted from a broken heart. Those who made the decision to end their own lives could not bear life in this world in the absence of the gift someone made them aware of, and they made the choice to depart it.

Depending on the intensity of the romantic desire one experiences, a distortion is created between the ideal world of that potential love and the physical world of reality and society that exists. To bridge that divide, tears must be shed. While they can be seen as the entry of love into our world, they can also be seen as emotional pushups. Whoever sheds them gains emotional strength. As an individual becomes emotionally stronger, they become kinder and more generous. They can bear more of the burden of the emotional pain that exists in this world and by doing so, they can be of greater service to others. As they increase their emotional strength, they can make greater and greater sacrifices for the sake of love.

Over the past few years, our society has been undergoing a great transition as those in the freedom movement have sacrificed emotionally for the sake of love. We have been outcast, belittled, insulted, and shunned from society. We have been treated as second class citizens and in various parts of the world, we have been banned from leaving our homes, banned from working, forced to cover our faces in public, and nagged nonstop to take a vaccine we believe has a good chance of being lethal.

We have lacked for love during this time, as the beautiful women of our planet have held off and observed while men have engaged in discourse with one another and worked towards the salvation of our species. They have seen where these men have been good and just, and they have seen where they have been cruel and gross. Yet, they have continued living their lives according to the rules that exist within our society and have not outwardly made great changes in their routines or beliefs.

But, they recognize truth as they observe this world. They put things out there when they feel like it, to trigger people or to express annoyance or pain or other emotions they want to express. But they are dissimilar from men, and they aren't revealing everything. They keep a lot hidden as they observe this evolution.

As they do, the desire for them amongst the men in the freedom movement grows. Their testosterone levels continue to increase, and women around the world continue to find themselves more enamored by these strong men who are willing to face emotional abuse for the sake of doing good in this world. Behind closed doors, they likely sneer at the obedient puppies licking their boots and attempting to please them with the bullying tactics that advanced them to the positions of political and social influence they have enjoyed.

The gasoline has been poured on the timber and each passing day, more timber and gasoline are added. All that is missing is a spark, and when that spark is lit, there will be a sort of collective orgasm that will announce our entry into heaven, and the surrender of the old order.

Metamorphosis is a phenomenon that exists throughout nature, as illustrated by the classic example of a caterpillar turning into a butterfly. Consciousness has long been considered by mystics to be an agent of creation and this is where I believe entropy will get turned on its head. The idea that the universe is approaching thermal equilibrium can be restated as saying the order of our current universe is descending into chaos. But it is not the order of the universe that is descending into chaos, it is only the order of society.

If I approach a messy table, I can choose to place the items into an order so that I may more easily find them. I can reduce the

116

work that I need to do in the future to accomplish the tasks that I have set for myself. I can do so through the power of consciousness.

I expect that when our joyous conclusion arrives, a physical metamorphosis will also occur for those involved with the process. I believe we will become as angels and begin to emit light that is produced by our own consciousness. I also believe we will sprout wings, and I believe we will use those wings to store information.

Information must be stored in a physical medium and wings can provide such a medium, for the memory of our brains will be insufficient. When someone surrenders romantically, the thing they are surrendering is information. They are offering the missing information that has been sought after, the prize that has aroused the desire of the other.

I expect this prize will be stored in our wings because I find it too convenient that so many different cultures would describe such beings if they did not exist, and because I believe self-similarity is a consistent phenomenon in our universe. I do not believe I was the first being to fall completely in love, and I do not believe I will be the first to manifest that love. I believe that upon the realization of the love that is approaching, our species will join a heavenly host and a galactic hoard that can become an amazing trading partner.

Our planet is still rich in natural resources that may well be depleted in other parts of the galaxy. An element like platinum, which has the highest melting point of any known element, could have an extraordinarily high value to an alien species. What technology might they share with us in exchange for mining rights to some of that platinum? What might our oil be worth to them? Our silver? Our gold? Free trade benefits both parties of the trade that takes place and having access to the trades offered by the angels will greatly increase our standard of living.

Death

It has been said that death and taxes are the only sure things in life but in this book, I have outlined how society might get by without taxes. Is it possible that death might also be avoided?

During my episode in 2018, I found myself in a situation where I felt like I briefly crossed the threshold of death and had a choice to either remain here or to transition to heaven. I was eligible to go to heaven because I understood the rules to exist within heaven, but I chose to remain here as an act of service to my fellow humans. As someone who understood the economics of this world well, I felt I was in a unique position to build a bridge between heaven and Earth, and I resolved to do so, despite the dreadful suffering that one experiences while existing here.

In the years since that moment, I have focused on increasing my understanding of many topics and on being of service to God and my fellow humans. This process has been emotionally painful, and I have shed many tears over this time, increasing my emotional strength and gradually bringing love into manifestation here.

We have come a long way as a species. A few years ago, people in the freedom movement seemed far more susceptible to people pleasing than they are now as they resorted to tired and futile moral claims. A person in the movement who blocked me years ago later unblocked me, and we have found ways to inspire each other as this struggle has continued. We have learned to shed tears and to strengthen, and we have found reasons to carry on the struggle.

For me, my children have been my greatest strength, and it has been for their sake that I have continued here, rather than choosing to depart this world. The romantic love that I desire gives me insufficient reason to stay here, for I expect if I depart from this world, I will cross the gates of heaven, and the love I long for will await me there. It is instead my love for my children that has kept me here. That is the love for which I have sacrificed.

A story is unfolding during my time here and if our planet can achieve a heavenly status, perhaps there will cease to be a need for death. By resurrecting Jesus, God and the heavenly host have shown us such a miracle is possible. Perhaps death has simply been a gift we have been promised as an act of kindness from our creator, an escape from a painful world when we can no longer find the inspiration to face it. But perhaps, just as Jesus was resurrected, so too can those of us here be protected from death once we have joined that heavenly host.

Even if not, and we are destined for death, and I am mistaken about the spirit continuing afterward, I will continue to carry on here for as long as my body allows it. I will continue to offer my will and my life over to the care of God as I understand God, I will continue to place one foot in front of the other, and I will continue to strive to make this a better world for my children, for the others suffering in this world, and for future generations. I will praise God for the experiences I've had, the joys that I've imagined, and the fantasies I've known. I will thank him for the promise, and I will hope that somewhere in this universe, that promise may be realized, for it is a beautiful promise and it is good if such beauty exists in this universe, regardless of how much of it I am able to perceive.

Recommendations

Throughout this book, I have discussed societal solutions and an outlook for the future, but I have offered little in the way of individual advice. In this section, I will do so.

Each one of us is on a physical, intellectual, emotional, and spiritual journey and people should take actions based on where they are in these various journeys.

The most significant journey for me has been the spiritual journey, and for me it has come down to deciding to turn my will and my life over to God as I understand God. With this said, different people have different beliefs regarding God, and my own interpretation has evolved over time. In addition to surrendering to God, there are other aspects to spirituality including self-reflection, atoning for one's sins, and being of service towards others. All of these can be explored as spiritual solutions and upon enlisting in God's spiritual army, the spiritual journey he puts each of us on is unique.

To determine whether one has work to do in the spiritual realm, one might ask oneself if they are at ease with the universe around them. Do they accept the world around them as it is, acknowledge that perhaps not all is as they wish it would be, but feel as though they have done everything within their power to improve it? People should ask themselves this question and if the answer is no, they should ask themselves what they can do to change it to a yes.

This may require sacrifice. The spiritual journey has not been an easy one for me and I do not know how difficult it will be for you (assuming God accepts you into his ranks) but if you want to become an angel, I'm confident you'll need to behave like one.

If you are at a loss as to what action to take in your spiritual journey and you like the ideas I present in this book, you can be of service to me and the rest of humanity by helping me distribute this book as widely as possible. The book will be available for sale on my website www.humandiscourse.com and by referring people there, you can expose them to this book, as well as the other resources available there. You can distribute business cards in a busy area sending people to my website. You can order a custom bumper sticker with a slogan that you think will draw people there. The possibilities for slogans you might use are endless but one I have used is "Why am I unvaccinated? Find out at www.humandiscourse.com."

Once the spiritual journey has been undertaken, the physical journey is only a matter of time and effort. It's walking the path every day to achieve the spiritual objectives that one is assigned by God. At some point in the journey, the physical action to take will likely be confession, and this is where the emotional journey will begin.

If we want to be loved, we will need to be trusted, and trust takes time to develop. The first step is to acknowledge where we have been dishonest or exhibited other defects of character that have hurt others. In these circumstances, we need to acknowledge our wrongdoing and set out to correct whatever harm we have done.

In addition to trusting us, other people will also need to become aware of our heart's desires. It is extremely unlikely that anyone will give us what we want if they don't know what that is. It is important to be authentic, but it is also important to use discretion and to only confess things to people we trust. It would be a great shame if people gained private information about us and used it to publicly ridicule or otherwise torment us. Personal confessions can be difficult to make for this reason, but we will find that once our desire becomes strong enough, we are faced with little choice. To confess is to open ourselves up to painful possibilities, but not to confess is to deny ourselves any possibility of getting what we ultimately want.

In our society, many feelings are a degree of taboo to express including sexual desires towards someone of the same sex, someone who is married, someone in the workplace, a transgender person, someone of another race or nationality, someone who is substantially older or younger, or someone from a different political party. Because of this, the immediate reaction

121

to one's confession is often likely to be rejection, and this rejection will cause emotional pain.

In some circumstances, the rejection may be a kneejerk reaction that is later amended once the recipient has time to consider the information. In other circumstances, the rejection will be final. We may experience a torture of not knowing which it is, and we may need to shed many tears to gain the emotional strength just to carry on our daily lives.

Recall that with every tear shed, love is being brought into this world. Your pain is real, and it is worthy of acknowledgement, even if others have judged you unworthy of the joy you seek. Through feeling the pain and shedding the tears, your humanity will be revealed. Your tears will soften you, and you will start to increase your capacity for kindness, as I described in the section on angels.

Our minds exist to figure out the solutions to our problems and the problem that your mind will seek to solve upon your rejection will be why you were rejected. Perhaps the individual offering the rejection will offer some insight and no doubt, you will read into every word they say to try to figure it out. But more likely than not, their explanations will be dissatisfactory, and your mind will be left searching for an answer.

The answers for you are likely to be different than the answers were for me because your circumstances and your spiritual mission will be different. Each individual is different, and each has their unique demands. Despite this, a lot of general romantic advice can be found online, and I highly recommend seeking out these resources. You can also watch my videos and read my blog at www.humandiscourse.com to bear witness to some of the mental anguish I have gone through on my own journey. While our circumstances may differ, seeing my path might offer you some encouragement and give a voice to some of the feelings you may be feeling but have not yet found the words to express.

My videos are probably not for everyone, and neither may be my blog. I do not know who the ultimate audience of these materials will be, just as I do not know who the ultimate audience of this book will be. I do encourage each of you to check out at least a few different videos because my emotional states and subject matter differ greatly from one video to the next, and there may be some you will obtain value from, even if it is not all of them.

While the attainment of our spiritual and romantic objectives is important, we also live in a material world in which survival is not guaranteed at this time. As we go about our lives, we find we have responsibilities to tend to and these responsibilities can at time remove us far from our desired destination in an intellectual, physical, and emotional sense.

Yet, all the intermediate steps required are a part of the journey towards one's ultimate objectives. God assigns us the work that is in front of us, and we choose whether to do that work or give up on the journey. My hope is that this book will provide a roadmap for society to transition to freedom and thereby provide individuals with paths to walk where there are clear destinations in sight and foreseeable ways of getting to them.

The path will look different for everyone. Based on your location, assets, relationships, physical characteristics, and skills, your opportunities in a free society will look different. Perhaps you will work in construction on a new factory, become an agricultural worker, or become an accountant. Perhaps you will become an independent drug distributor, an independent taxi driver, or a general laborer who finds a new gig each morning. Perhaps you will work for the government's liquidation estate, as a private security agent, or as an administrator of justice on the behalf of others. Perhaps you will provide childcare for children, a maid service for money, or work for a charity. Perhaps you will be a mediator, work for a private regulator, or become a sex worker.

In a free society, there will be hope for everyone, and my intention in writing this book has been to offer that hope to the world. Even someone who has already made the unfortunate decision to get jabbed may place hope in the chance that whatever was injected into them was not a biological agent that will mutate and progressively attack their immune system over time. It may well be that the "kill shot" has not yet been issued and will not be until they estimate they have maximized compliance amongst the population.

Or it may be that the mistake made was a critical one that will terminate your existence in this body. If that is the case, hopefully I have at least elucidated how a free society can work and how a heavenly existence can be manifested. If you understand the rules of behavior by which people should live, then you should have no fear of death, for God would surely be thrilled to welcome more people to heaven who understand and play by the rules, even if their welcome occurs posthumously.

Until we get a free society, we must acknowledge the reality of the rules of the societal structure that exists around us. While we may consider these rules to be unjust, we should still acknowledge the likely consequences that exist for our behavior. There is a lot of talk of rebellion among freedom supporters, but each act of rebellion should be considered independently with a risk-reward analysis. It will do the freedom movement little good if all its strongest supporters end up imprisoned and unable to effectually spread the message of freedom because the government found them in violation of their laws. Regardless of how unjust a law may be, a person who doesn't support it can end up just as trapped within a jail cell for breaking it as someone who does.

Until we get freedom, we are playing a game of survival. Inflation continues to worsen and there's no reason to expect this trend will reverse until the U.S. dollar has become entirely worthless. Governments are taking drastic action to attempt to cripple dissenters economically and as they do so, more people in our society are becoming more desperate. We should expect that at some point, people who are being told to remain in their homes and not to work while inflation soars will reach a breaking point. When this occurs, we can expect the incidents of violence

124

in our society to increase, while the number of those opposing the current structures of power does the same.

At some point, there will be a critical mass of government supporters who jump off the government bandwagon and begin to seek a new God. This may occur once the vaccines are determined to be killing people or it may come when people discover there's no more food to purchase at the store. When it happens, people will likely panic and resort to whatever means are necessary to feed themselves. Those who have prepared for this eventuality will need to be locked, loaded, and prepared to defend what is theirs.

When faced with the reality of an armed population willing to defend their property from theft, it is likely that the former government supporters will give up their attempts to control people and steal their property. They will face the reality of starvation behind them and a loaded gun in front of them. It is at this point that I expect they will become hopeless, and in the shadow of this hopelessness, perhaps my book can offer them a new hope. Then, perhaps they will grant us our freedom and we can get to work hiring people and rebuilding our world from the ground up.

Afterword

Thank you for reading my book. I hope I have offered insights that help you in your journey, and us in our collective journey towards freedom. There are doubtlessly societal problems I did not touch on and perspectives I did not consider in the authoring of this book, despite my attempts to make my voice as broad as possible through incorporating the lessons I've learned listening to my fellow humans. The human discourse is never truly complete, and I welcome discussions relating to the topics contained in this book and any other societal issues that people find of interest. I am just a single man, but I believe with the diverse knowledge and skillsets that exist within our species, we can solve any problem we are faced with. I wish each one of you the best, despite any ill will you may have felt towards me over the past few years, and despite the ways that you may have negatively judged my behavior. I wish no harm upon anyone on this planet, for I too am imperfect and in a grand sense, every outcome in this universe depends greatly on good fortune. Despite all the sacrifices I have made, I'm an incredibly fortunate soul.

I invite you to check out my website www.humandiscourse.com where I list various commentators who I feel offer valuable insight, along with a blog I wrote, links to my YouTube channels, and a couple lengthy discussions I have participated in. Regardless of whether you check out my additional materials, I hope you find the answers you're looking for so that someday, we might look across at one another and have laugh as we realize we're in heaven.

Appendix – Proposed Mandates of the First Security Force of the Free World (FSFFW)

1. The FSFFW will be funded solely through voluntary donations. No individual or organization will be compelled under violent threat to offer funding to this organization.

2. The FSFFW will enforce rules on the land, in the sea and in the air for the territory of the free world. The free world will consist of the former United States and its territories, in addition to any other nations that determine to become free through a dissolution and liquidation of their government, providing that greater than fifty percent of the formerly legal population of this additional territory consents to this expansion of the national security force, as determined by vote.

3. The FSFFW will act to prevent the following behaviors:

   a. Unwelcome touching of another individual's body that has not been authorized by the landowner

   b. Threats to touch another individual's body in unwelcome ways that have not been authorized by the landowner

   c. Attempts by a landowner to confine other people to their land

   d. Attempts to steal another person's property

   e. Attempts to vandalize another person's property

   f. Trespassing

   g. Sexual relations with a minor under the democratically decided age of consent

   h. Abortions occurring after the democratically decided age of life

   i. Using airspace without registering one's flight with the centralized air traffic control authority

j. Using a harbor without following the instructions of the harbor authority

k. Possessing nuclear material without allowing inspection and access by the international nuclear authority

l. Aggression against animals that has been voted by FSFFW contributors as enforceable. Through yes or no vote, contributors will determine whether the following classes of animals should be protected. Once a class of animal has been voted on as protected by the FSFFW, complaints of abuse against animals in that category will be investigated and the potential abusers will be tried in a similar manner as other criminals, with the exception that removal of the abused animal(s) and donation to an appropriate animal shelter will be added as an available punishment.

   1. Animals held as pets

   2. Wild animals that exist on someone's property

   3. Animals used in circuses

   4. Zoo animals

   5. Animals raised for meat and other products such as wool, milk and leather

   6. Animals used in other enterprises

m. An exception shall be made to the enforcement of unwelcome touch and threats for legacy charitable prisons that take over the government's population of violent criminals deemed a threat to society. The population transitioning to this prison system will be a percentage of the former prison population of that government that is the percentage determined by the vote of the funders of the FSFFW.

4. Property rights should be initially assigned in accordance with former ownership under the former jurisdiction and

reassigned based upon the voluntary transactions of members of society.

5. No landowner should be subjected to rules of a zoning authority except:

    a. Those rules that existed under the previous regime, and that have been democratically agreed to by the majority vote of the landowners of the zone, with each property owner having a single vote for each prior parcel of land they owned within that zone.

    b. Those rules that are unanimously agreed to by owners of land parcels within a zone.

6. If landowners unanimously agree to join a homeowners' association that will have certain authority over the land of the homeowners, they may do so and the FSFFW will protect the agreed-to rights of the homeowner's association. Homeowner's associations that existed in the prior regime will be continue to be recognized by the FSFFW.

7. When a criminal is apprehended in the act of a forbidden behavior, their punishment should be voted on by contributing members of the FSFFW. The members may either vote directly on each case or assign a third party to vote on their behalf.

8. The FSFFW will not be engaged to administer justice beyond that assigned to criminals caught in the act.

9. Voting rights will be granted to contributing donors to the FSFFW in proportion to their donation.

10. Elections will occur annually where contributors can vote on the age of consent, the age of life, and animal protections

11. When an individual is apprehended for a crime that the FSFFW has responded to, the individual will be detained by the FSFFW for a period of no longer than 30 days (90 days for cases involving a death) in which voting contributors can vote

on their punishment. If the majority votes for death, the individual will be executed using the most humane method available. If people vote for jail time or exile, they will also vote for the length of that sentence and the median vote will be used to determine it.

12. The FSFFW may sentence prisoners to sentences in prisons that it operates itself or by charitably funded prisons like the ones used to house legacy old-system prisoners deemed too great a threat to society to be set free.

13. Each prison in society, whether used to house FSFFW convicts or legacy prisoners of the old system, will be inspected annually by the FSFFW with the results posted to their website and public comments allowed. Upon a review of this material, FSFFW contributors will have a chance to vote on whether they consider than prison to be humane. Prisons deemed to be inhumane will have one month to provide a report on how they will correct their deficiencies at which point the voters will again vote on whether that prison should be continued. If the plan is dissatisfactory to the voters, the prisoners will be transported to a more humane facility as soon as possible. If a prison is voted as inhumane in more than one annual vote within a 5 year period, those prisoners will also be transported to a more human facility, even if the prison was able to come up with a satisfactory plan following its first infraction.

14. If individuals report crimes and when the FSFFW arrives, they determine there is no crime underway or evidence of a crime recently underway, that individual will be listed on the FSFFW's website as a false accuser. Testimonies from relevant parties will be posted to the website and voting members will be able to vote on whether the individual has abused their use of the FSFFW. If a majority vote determines that they have, the FSFFW will no longer respond to their calls for help. If an individual believes they have been unfairly accused as a false accuser, they may add additional testimony on an annual basis

to discuss their reforms and attempt to sway the vote in their favor.

15. Everyone who desires to utilize the FSFFW as a security service will need to register their name, picture, and a list of their real property holdings with the FSFFW.

16. No individual will be compelled to register with the FSFFW but no individual will be prevented from doing so unless they have been voted on as a false accuser.

17. The leader of the FSFFW will be voted on annually by vote of the contributors. This individual will be responsible for:

    a. Overseeing the addition of additional territories to FSFFW's jurisdiction through friendly discourse with foreign parties and seeking to gain consent for the FSFFW to expand into their territory through majority consent

    b. Overseeing the democratic processes required to administer the FSFFW

        1. The leader may determine what questions will be voted on through the election with relation to animal rights.

        2. The leader may not add any other questions to the vote that will determine the morality enforced by the organization.

        3. The leader may not cancel the other voting processes established in this document.

        4. Overseeing the enforcement against prohibited behavior

        5. Overseeing the administration of justice against those caught in the act

        6. Determining the length (up to 30 days or 90 days for cases involving a death) that a person

should be detained while voters decide upon their fate

    7. Determining what other individuals are hired to assist the leader with their duties

  c. Managing the budget of the FSFFW

    1. Any excess funds received by the organization beyond that needed for one year of future operations will be returned pro-rata to contributors from the previous year.

    2. If there is a shortfall in funds, the leader of the FSFFW should determine which services should be cut and which calls for help should not be responded to.

18. Any individual contributor can run for the office of leader, resulting in a likelihood that many candidates will seek the office. Whichever candidate receives the most votes will become the leader, regardless of how low a percentage of the population that is.

19. The leader's pay and the budget for other salaries will be voted on by contributing members annually.

20. If a leader of the FSFFW, while in office, is accused and convicted by majority vote of violating any of the provisions that the FSFFW is mandated to prevent, a recall election will take place to give the voting population a chance to pick a new leader. If someone who has previously been convicted of such desires to run for the position of leader, they may do so, but the circumstances of their previous issues will be available for the voting population to see.

21. If additional issues arise that require a modification to the mandates of the FSFFW, the change may be made through a 75% vote of donators.

About the Author

Nicholas Blakiston is an accountant, poker player, Phoenix Suns fan, Arizona Cardinals fan, occasional improv artist, former Navy nuclear electrician, black belt in Tae Kwon Do that he hasn't practiced for 20 years, former boy at an all-boys English boarding school named Sunningdale, and the son of legendary children's entertainer Roger Blakiston, better known by his stage name "Jolly Roger".

Roger Blakiston is the son of the Reverend Patrick Blakiston, a deceased English clergyman who was the fifth generation of clergymen in his family. The Reverend Patrick was married for over fifty years to his wife, Rosemary Blakiston, who lived to be a hundred years old before finally passing away in 2013.

During the blitz of London during World War II, Rosemary Blakiston (then Rosemary Easton) volunteered to move to London and to work as a children's nurse to assist in the war effort. Soon after the completion of the war, she married Patrick and they would have three children.

In addition to Nicholas' father, Rosemary and Patrick had two daughters, Padmasuri (formerly Hilary Blakiston) who became a Buddhist and Philippa Timewell (formerly Philippa Blakiston), a free thinker who remains in fairly regular email communication with Nicholas.

Nicholas' mother, Carol Blakiston, is of Polish descent and has worked as a nurse for most of her adult life outside of her children's early years. Her father was a Chief Quartermaster in the United States Navy, a service that her brother Ed and her son Nicholas would also spend some time in. Her mother was a factory worker for General Electric.

Nicholas' parents met on a cruise ship where his father was employed as a magician. They fell in love and she ended up joining his magic act as he performed a six-month gig in Australia. They would then move to New York City and get married before relocating to England a year later.

Their first child, Daniel Blakiston, would pass away from a heart defect at a year old. Nicholas Blakiston was born a couple years later and would be followed by two sisters, Rebecca and Jessica. Rebecca is a librarian working at the University of Arizona while Jessica works in marketing for Amazon.

Nicholas has two children who at the time of this publication are eight-year-old Annabelle and six-year-old Henry. Annabelle recently made the Principal's List at school and Henry can do a backwards dive when the swimming pool is warm enough.

Despite the differences in spiritual and life philosophies within the family, the members have managed to find occasional common ground, frequent mutual respect and very occasional mutual understanding.

Nicholas is divorced and taking some time to consider his romantic options.